Praise for *Smart Chicken*

"In this excellent series of cookbooks, Jane Kinderlehrer, former food editor of *Prevention* magazine, shares with readers her lifetime-tested recipes for heavenly, healthful eating. *Smart Chicken* offers mouth-watering poultry dishes and accompaniments that are low in fat, sodium, and calories and high in fiber, protein and flavor."—*Book News*

"The recipes are inventive, easy, and can be used as is or adapted to meet the special dietary needs of bodybuilders. They're good-tasting too." —Anne Marie Riccitelli, *Female Body Building*

"This little volume hits everyday favorites (roast chicken with lemon and wine, roast chicken with rosemary and garlic) as well as the unusual grapefruit chicken." —Beverly Bundy, *Fort Worth Star Telegram*

"The format is attractive and easy to follow…. Jane Kinderlehrer has put together a wide variety of dishes that are interesting but not difficult to prepare." —*Kliatt*

Praise for *Smart Fish*

"This tasteful and simple collection of 101 kitchen-tested recipes…not only steers you to delicious and nutritious eating, but also gives you the facts you need to be informed about fish safety."
—*The International Cookbook Revue*

"Here are oceans of low-calorie, low-fat, extremely healthy recipes for main courses, soups and salads that will turn the tide in your family to eat smart." —*The Doubleday Health Book Club*

The Smart Chicken & Fish Cookbook

Over 200 Delicious and Nutritious Recipes for Main Courses, Soups, and Salads

JANE KINDERLEHRER

NEWMARKET PRESS

New York

THE NEWMARKET JANE KINDERLEHRER SMART FOOD SERIES

Dedicated to my sister, Betty Kane, and my brother, Harry Arden, in nostalgic recollection of the many chicken dinners we have so happily shared, and to the memory of my brother Irwin Arden, who taught me how to fish.

First Edition

10 9 8 7 6 5 4 3 2 1

Library of Congress Cataloging-in-Publication Data

Kinderlehrer, Jane.
The smart chicken & fish cookbook : over 200 delicious and nutritious recipes for
main courses, soups, and salads / Jane Kinderlehrer. — 1st ed.
p. cm. — (The Newmarket Jane Kinderlehrer smart food series)
Includes index.
ISBN 1-55704-544-5
1. Cookery (Chicken) 2. Cookery (Fish) 3. Low-calorie diet — Recipes.
I. Title. II. Series.
TX750.5.C45 K5623 2002
641.6'65 — dc21
2002009795

Quantity Purchases
Companies, professional groups, clubs, and other organizations may qualify for special
terms when ordering quantities of this title. For information, contact: Special Sales Dept.,
Newmarket Press, 18 East 48th Street, New York, New York 10017, call (212) 832-3575, or
e-mail mailbox@newmarketpress.com.

Book design by
Manufactured in the United States

www.newmarketpress.com

Contents

Part One—Smart Chicken

Part Two—Smart Fish

xii

METRIC CONVERSION CHART

1 teaspoon = 5 ml.   1 tablespoon = 15 ml.
1 ounce = 30 ml.   1 cup = 240 ml./.24 l.
1 quart = 950 ml./.95 l.   1 gallon = 3.80 l.

1 ounce = 28 gr.   1 pound = 454 gr./.454 kg.

F° 200 225 250 275 300 325 350 375 400 425 450
C° 93 107 121 135 149 163 177 191 204 218 232

ABBREVIATIONS

cal = calories   sat = saturated
pro = protein   unsat = unsaturated
g = gram   chol = cholesterol
mg = milligram   tr = trace

Part One

Smart Chicken

INTRODUCTION

Chicken Every
Sunday, Monday, Tuesday . . .

Remember when "chicken in every pot" and "chicken every Sunday" were the hallmarks of "prosperity"? That was long ago, when chicken, because of its succulent goodness, was everybody's favorite special occasion meal.

It still is. But because of our current concern over the danger of cholesterol-raising saturated fats, chicken and its cousins in the fowl family have won new prestige and a favored spot on the menu.

Chicken is a smart choice not just for special occasions but also for every day of the week. Poultry is less costly, less fatty, and higher in nutritional value in proportion to calories than either beef or lamb. And though chicken's succulence makes it taste like a zillion calories, it's actually a great food to lose weight on while enjoying the pleasures of the palate.

The usual portion of 3½ ounces of chicken or turkey provides only 150 calories (slightly more for dark meat), plus an impressive 28 to 31 grams of protein (about half the usual adult daily requirement), as well as potassium, iron, phosphorus, and calcium. Chicken also contains vitamin A. Both chicken and turkey have some B vitamins, with a significant content of the cholesterol-lowering B vitamin niacin.

3

And with 101 quick and easy "smart" recipes to choose from, chicken three times a week or even every day need never be boring. On the contrary, you'll find that your chicken dinners with their heavenly cooking aromas will enhance your family's joy of eating.

Ounce for ounce, chicken contains as much protein as red meat, but with far less fat. And the fat in chicken is not the cholesterol-raising saturated type. Far from it! The fat in chicken is predominantly heart-healthy monounsaturated, which means that chicken skin is not the cholesterol-raising villain many people believe it to be. Chicken skin is only 17 percent fat and, when rendered, can add the most delectable of flavors and irresistible crunch to some of my favorite dishes, such as chopped liver and potato knishes. (See Index listing for specific recipes.)

Chicken is so versatile, there's something about it to please everyone at the table, even the picky eater. There's dark and white meat; there are drumsticks, wings, thighs, and breasts, each with a unique flavor and texture.

However, not all chicken dinners are smart.

A chicken dinner is smart when it is low in fat, low in sodium, low in calories, and served with high-fiber accompaniments.

For instance, a 3½-ounce serving of processed chicken nuggets can contain as much as 323 calories, 20 grams of fat, and 512 milligrams of sodium. A boneless chicken breast that is steamed, baked, or sautéed contains just 173 calories, 4½ grams of fat, and 77 milligrams of sodium.

The uses of chicken are countless. Its succulence can be part of every meal except dessert.

As the nineteenth-century French gastronome Jean Anthelme Brillat-Savarin wrote, "Poultry is for the cook what canvas is to the painter. It is served to us boiled, roasted, fried, hot or cold, whole or

4

in pieces, with or without sauce, boned, skinned, stuffed, and always with equal success."

With this book as your guide, you can perfect your technique with all these methods, prepare a variety of delectable meals with ease and pizzazz, and make them all smart.

MEET THE MEMBERS OF THE POULTRY FAMILY

Cornish hens. Also called Rock Cornish hens. A young, small chicken that weighs ¾ to 1½ pounds—tender, juicy meat—great for roasting and also very tasty braised, broiled, or fried.

Broilers. The terms "broiler" and "fryer" are frequently used interchangeably, but a broiler may weigh a little less than a fryer— about 2 to 3 pounds—and is often sold as a "split."

Fryers. Slightly larger than broilers, weighing 3 to 4 pounds, and sometimes called broiler-fryers. They're sold whole, quartered, or cut into serving pieces.

Pullets. Small roasters—4 to 5 pounds—designated mostly for the roasting or stewing pan.

Roasters. Larger chickens, usually served whole—now available in 5- to 7-pound sizes. They carve nicely. Roaster parts are also marketed separately.

Stewing chickens. Older, larger, and tougher but richer in flavor. Weighing about 6 pounds, they're great for soups, stewing, fricassee, or chicken pot pie.

Capons. Very flavorful, tender, and juicy, these large and meaty castrated roosters may weigh 6 to 12 pounds. Superb for roasting.

Duck—broiler-fryer. Very young (under 8 weeks old), less than 3 pounds, excellent fried or broiled.

Duck—roaster. Eight to 16 weeks old, fatty and tender—best roasted or braised.

Goose. All meat is dark and fatty. When 4 to 12 pounds, it is best roasted. When over 12 pounds, it's best braised.

Squab. Domesticated pigeon weighing less than 1 pound. Excellent roasted or braised.

Turkey—fryer-roaster. Small (4 to 9 pounds), young, and tender, with smooth skin and flexible breastbone; excellent broiled, oven-fried, or roasted.

Turkey—young. Usually 7 to 15 pounds, best when roasted.

Turkey—yearling. Twenty to 30 pounds, usually roasted or braised.

SMART TIPS FOR CLEVER COOKS

Most recipes for the preparation of poultry call for added fat in the stuffing and on the bird. The new dietary guidelines state that no more than 30 percent of the calories should be derived from fat. Many physicians are advising no more than 20 percent as a preventative measure and no more than 15 percent as a therapeutic measure for those who already have cardiovascular problems.

To skin or not to skin: Does removing the skin before cooking chicken cut down on fat? No, according to researchers from the University of Minnesota. They found that it doesn't matter much whether you remove the skin before or after cooking. Even though about half the fat in poultry comes from the skin, apparently no significant amount is transferred to the meat during cooking. Skinning poultry before cooking only leads to drier—not leaner—meat, the researchers found.

Here are some tips to help you reduce the fat and savor the flavor:

- Cut away the visible fat and extra skin from chicken and other poultry before cooking, but do not discard it. Render it. (See the recipe for chicken fat.) Use the rendered chicken fat (schmaltz) to enhance the flavor of many poultry dishes. Chicken fat is a far better cooking fat than butter if you're concerned about cholesterol.

- Sauté onions for the poultry dressing without fat. Here's how: Use a tiny bit of water, just enough to barely cover the bottom of a large pan. Add onions and turn up the heat. When water begins to boil, cover the pan with a tight-fitting lid and lower the heat to medium for about 10 to 15 minutes. The onions will be nicely sautéed and sweet-tasting. Or microwave the onions with a little water or chicken broth, but without fat, for about 2 minutes on high.

- Follow the same procedure for garlic and julienned vegetables.

- To make a sauce that needs a glaze, remove the onions when they are ready. Take a teaspoon of arrowroot powder or cornstarch and dissolve with a teaspoon of water. Stir until thickened. Add spices, herbs, and juices to flavor the sauce.

- To sauté chicken or turkey without fat, place in a sauté pan with 2 ice cubes and stir constantly to prevent sticking.

- Sauté thinly sliced vegetables such as yellow squash, zucchini, peppers, and onions in 2 tablespoons of tomato juice. Toss with herbs such as thyme, basil, and oregano and serve as a side dish. A delicious source of fiber.

- Save the renderings in the bottom of the broiler or roaster pan to make a natural gravy without added fat. To degrease the renderings quickly, place them in a measuring cup. Then submerge the cup in ice water three-quarters of the way up. The fat will rise to the top and begin to thicken, allowing you to skim it off easily. Or place the bowl of drippings in the freezer for 10 minutes, then skim off the hardened fat that rises to the surface. Reheat the remaining juices, and season with herbs and spices to taste.

- To thicken gravy, first skim off excess fat from the pan drippings. Combine 2 tablespoons of flour with 1 cup of water or stock, and blend in a screw-top jar or in a blender or food processor. Add the flour mixture to the pan drippings and stir constantly over medium heat until thickened.

- When you're reheating meat, keep it moist and flavorful without adding fat. Place a lettuce leaf in the bottom of a casserole or pie plate, then place the meat on the lettuce and cover with another lettuce leaf. Add a tiny bit of water or broth to the bottom of the pan and heat at 350 degrees until the meat is heated through.

- Many recipes call for fats to thicken a soup base. Instead, try boiling potatoes, puréeing them, and using this purée as a thickener. Other puréed vegetables can also be used, not only as thickeners but also as flavor and nutrient enhancers.

HELPFUL HINTS

- To freeze fresh poultry, remove the store wrapping and rinse the poultry in cold water. Pat dry with paper towels, then wrap in freezer paper, heavy-duty foil, or plastic wrap. Label each package, noting the date, which parts are included, how many pieces, and where it is placed in the freezer. It will keep up to 6 months.

- Hard-frozen poultry can go right from the store into your freezer without rewrapping. Do not allow it to thaw at all.

- If it has thawed in the store or in getting it home, cook it promptly and then freeze it or use it.

- Never refreeze thawed, uncooked chicken.

- If you're making a stew, chicken can go right into the pot from the freezer.

- If you're using it for fried, broiled, barbecued, or roasted dishes, thaw it first. It will cook more evenly.

- If a recipe calls for bread crumbs, remember that one standard-size slice of bread will yield ½ to ¾ cup of fresh bread crumbs. That same slice of bread when dried will yield about 3 to 4 tablespoons of dried bread crumbs. Use about half the amount of dried crumbs as a replacement for fresh crumbs.

- To broil chicken successfully, place the chicken on the rack of a broiler pan and broil 4 to 7 inches from heat, turning and basting frequently until chicken is tender, usually in about 40 minutes. To glaze, brush chicken with the glaze during the last 20 minutes.

- When a recipe calls for pounding chicken cutlets to flatten them to a uniform thickness, place the cutlets between two sheets of waxed paper and pound with the bottom of a skillet.

- When a recipe calls for sautéeing onions with fat, you can eliminate the fat by using a little chicken or vegetable broth, or by using the microwave on full power for about 2 minutes for 3 tablespoons of chopped onions, covered.

- Many recipes call for herbal seasoning. This is available commercially (for example, Mrs. Dash, Herbal Bouquet, or Spike) or you can make your own and use it in place of salt.

HERBAL SEASONING

⅛ teaspoon cayenne powder
¼ teaspoon garlic powder
1 tablespoon dried parsley
½ teaspoon paprika
½ teaspoon dried thyme

½ teaspoon dried marjoram
½ teaspoon onion powder
1 teaspoon roasted sesame
  seeds

Crush or blend in a seed mill or blender until powdery. Place in a shaker topped jar.

1

CHICKEN SALADS

For lunch, brunch, a buffet spread, or a take-along dish for a special occasion, chicken salad is a popular choice. It's the perfect way to use leftover chicken or turkey without subjecting its nutrients to more heat.

Go creative with your poultry salads. Vary the flavor and texture of your salads with crunchy almonds, walnuts, peanuts, or hazelnuts. Add to their succulence with grapes, peaches, pineapple, apples, raisins, or currants. Make it tantalizing with a touch of raspberry or balsamic vinegar in a piquant salad dressing. Stuff it in avocados or in red, yellow, or green peppers. Serve a small portion as a prelude to a sumptuous meal or a larger portion as an elegant, satisfying meal in itself.

Tropical Chicken Salad

A lovely medley of fruits and nuts makes this salad a melody of delightful flavors and textures.

2 cups cooked chicken, cut in bite-size pieces

1 cup diced celery

1 20-ounce can pineapple chunks, drained (retain juice)

2 oranges, peeled and sectioned

½ cup chopped pecans, lightly roasted

1 cup seedless grapes

4 tablespoons reduced-calorie mayonnaise combined with 4 tablespoons of the retained pineapple juice romaine lettuce leaves

Combine all ingredients except lettuce in a glass serving bowl. Serve on the lettuce leaves.

Yield: 6 servings. *Each serving provides: 220 cal, 16 g pro, 1.2 g sat fat, 7.2 g unsat fat, 46 mg chol.*

Waldorf Chicken Salad

This perennial favorite, moistened with tofu mayonnaise, features tart apples and sweet grapes—a very tasty combo that provides both vitamin C and fiber.

2 cups cooked chicken, cut in bite-size pieces

1 large Granny Smith apple, unpeeled

2 stalks celery, sliced diagonally

1 small green or red pepper, diced

½ small onion, diced

1 cup seedless red or green grapes, cut in halves

½ cup walnuts, coarsely chopped

1 cup raisins

⅔ cup orange juice

½ cup soft tofu or plain yogurt

⅛ teaspoon ground nutmeg (optional)

dark green lettuce leaves

In a glass bowl, combine the chicken, apple, celery, pepper, onion, grapes, raisins, and half of the walnuts.

In a small bowl, beat with a fork the orange juice, yogurt or tofu, and nutmeg until well blended. Pour over the chicken mixture and mix well. Garnish with the remaining walnuts. Serve on the lettuce leaves.

Yield: 4 servings. *Each serving provides: 330 cal, 28 g pro, 1 g sat fat, 11.5 g unsat fat, 46 mg chol.*

Chicken Pasta Salad

Pasta with its complex carbohydrates marries very well with high-protein chicken, making this salad a satisfying, nutritious meal in itself. Delightful served on the patio when warm breezes are blowing.

¼ cup reduced-calorie mayonnaise or salad dressing
2 tablespoons chicken broth
½ teaspoon dried crushed thyme
½ teaspoon dill weed
1 teaspoon Dijon mustard
1 teaspoon herbal seasoning
2 cups cooked chicken, cut in bite-size chunks

1 cup corkscrew noodles, cooked and drained (about 2 cups cooked)
2 tablespoons oat bran
2 scallions, chopped
1 cup chopped tomato
1 cup green pepper, cut in chunks
dark green lettuce leaves

Combine the salad dressing, chicken broth, thyme, dill, mustard, and herbal seasoning. Mix well. Add the remaining ingredients except the lettuce leaves. Mix to combine the ingredients. Chill several hours before serving. Serve on the lettuce leaves.

Yield: 4 servings. *Each serving provides: 227 cal, 24 g pro, 1 g sat fat, 2 g unsat fat, 46 mg chol.*

Quickie Chicken Salad—Italian Style

A very popular, easy-to-assemble salad; great for a casual brunch or buffet.

3 cups cooked chicken, cut in bite-size chunks
1 cup chopped celery
1 (6-ounce) jar marinated artichoke hearts, drained
½ cup pitted ripe olives, drained and sliced

1 can (8 ounce) water chestnuts, drained and sliced
½ cup Italian dressing
dark green lettuce leaves
tomato wedges

Combine all the ingredients except the lettuce leaves and tomato wedges. Chill. Serve in a bowl lined with the lettuce leaves. Garnish with the tomato wedges.

Yield: 6 servings. *Each serving provides: 174 cal, 28 g pro, 11 g unsat fat, 50 mg chol.*

2

ROAST CHICKEN

Nothin' says lovin' like a roast chicken in the oven. I like to bring the roast chicken to the table in all its glory—uncut and majestic in its crisp brown overcoat. There's nothing like this presentation to get the salivary juices flowing.

Roasting is an easy and tasty way of preparing all kinds of young, tender poultry—chicken, game hen, turkey, duck, and goose.

First, to truss, pull the skin flaps over the body and neck cavities, and either sew the skin in place or use skewers. Tie the legs together, then fold the wings back and under the bird, and tie them close to the body.

Place whole poultry breast side up on a rack in a shallow pan. Roast at 325 to 350 degrees. Baste every 30 to 45 minutes. About 30 minutes before the bird is completely roasted, untie the trussed legs to facilitate browning of the under side of the legs.

Roast chickens can be simple or exotic accompanied or stuffed with fruits, vegetables, grains, or nuts. Approach the roasting of the bird with a creative gleam and a shelf full of herbs and spices.

Choose a large roaster or capon for 6 or more diners, and figure 15 to 20 minutes per pound in a 350-degree oven. Smaller chickens need about 25 minutes per pound.

16

To determine if the bird is ready for its grand entrance, pierce the thickest part of the thigh with a fork. The juices should be clear, without a trace of pink or red.

STUFFING THE BIRD

To stuff or not to stuff? That is the question. Is it better to pile this tasty mixture into the body cavity, or to bake it separately? Remember that there is a symbiotic relationship between the bird and the stuffing. Each contributes moisture and flavor to the other. If you opt for stuffing the bird, consider this new method, which makes for a fantastic presentation and keeps even the usually dry breast meat moist, tender, and flavorful, transforming a humdrum stuffed bird into elegant gourmet fare. The key is to insert the stuffing between the flesh and the skin.

Here's how: Slip your fingers between skin and flesh, starting at the neck. Work your way down, loosening the flesh over each breast, and then free the skin from the legs, leaving the skin attached at the very tips of the drumsticks.

Starting at the neck, push the filling under the skin with one hand and use the other hand on the outside of the bird to mold the stuffing into place. Stuff the drumsticks and thighs, then make a thick coating over the breasts. This will protect the breast meat from drying out. Then tuck the neck flap over the opening and tuck it securely under the bird. Place the bird in a roasting pan and then in a hot oven (about 400 degrees). After 10 minutes, lower the heat to 350 degrees. After about 30 minutes, baste frequently with the pan juices.

How much stuffing do you need? Figure 2 cups for a 4-pound chicken. Stuffing can be prepared and refrigerated a day ahead, but never stuff the bird until you are ready to put it in the oven. To be prepared for the usual enthusiasm for "more stuffing, please," it's a good idea to prepare extra stuffing and bake it in a casserole for about an hour along with the chicken.

Roast Chicken with Lemon and Wine

My family's favorite chicken recipe. It's simple, quick, moist, tender, and full of flavor. Serve with a tossed salad and sweet potato-apple-granola casserole.

1 whole chicken, about 3½ pounds	½ teaspoon dry mustard
juice of 1 lemon	¼ teaspoon crushed dry thyme
1 clove garlic, crushed	1¼ teaspoon dried sage .
½ teaspoon ground ginger	1 teaspoon paprika
	½ cup dry white wine

Preheat oven to 350°F.

Clean the chicken and pat it dry.

Sprinkle with the lemon juice and rub with the crushed garlic inside and out. Combine the spices in a shaker-top jar and sprinkle the mixture over the chicken, coating all surfaces.

Tie the legs together and place the chicken breast side up in the roasting pan. Add the wine.

Bake for 1¼ hours or until the juices run clear.

Yield: 4 servings. *Each serving provides: 244 cal, 42 g pro, 2 g sat fat, 5 g unsat fat, 157 mg chol, 146 mg sodium.*

Roast Chicken with Garlic, Apples, and Rutabagas

The apples, garlic, and rutabagas are roasted with the chicken, then mashed and served as a lovely, tasty accompaniment.

1   *roasting chicken, about 3 pounds*
2   *teaspoons paprika*
½   *teaspoon freshly ground pepper*
½   *teaspoon ground ginger*
½   *teaspoon dry mustard*
1   *teaspoon chicken fat or olive oil*

3   *medium-size apples, unpeeled, cored, and cut into eighths*
1   *large rutabaga, peeled and thinly sliced*
4   *cloves garlic, peeled*
3   *tablespoons lemon juice*

Preheat oven to 325°F.

Combine the paprika, pepper, ginger, and mustard, and rub the chicken with them, inside and out.

Place the chicken in a roasting pan. Arrange the apples, rutabagas, and garlic around the chicken, then sprinkle the lemon juice over all.

Roast until golden brown, about 1¼ hours. Baste several times with the pan juices.

When the juices run clear, remove the chicken to a serving platter. Skim the fat from the roasting pan, then mash the apples, rutabagas, and garlic together with the pan juices. Serve with the chicken in a separate bowl.

Yield: 4 servings. *Each serving provides: 370 cal, 40 g pro, 4 g sat fat, 13 g unsat fat, 80 mg chol, 190 mg sodium.*

Roast Capon with
Onions and Prunes

Capons are more meaty, more tender, and more flavorful than roasters. They are also more fatty. The accompanying onions and prunes are an excellent accompaniment, providing fiber and nutrients that help in the utilization of fats.

1 9- to 10-pound capon
   herbal seasoning and freshly
     ground pepper to taste
1 teaspoon paprika

1 clove garlic
½ pound seedless prunes
2 medium-size onions, peeled
2 cups water

Preheat oven to 425°F.

Soak the prunes in the water.

Rub the capon with the garlic, and sprinkle inside and out with the seasonings.

Place the capon on its side in a shallow roasting pan and scatter the onions, gizzard, and neck around it.

Roast for 20 minutes and turn the capon on its other side.

Roast the capon, basting frequently 20 minutes longer, and turn the bird on its back.

Roast, basting, for another 20 minutes.

Reduce the oven heat to 350°F. Add the prunes. Cover the breast of the capon with foil, and continue roasting and basting for 30 minutes longer.

Pour off the fat from the roasting pan, and place the pan on the stove. Add the water in which the prunes were soaked, and stir with a wooden spoon to dissolve the brown particles that cling to the bottom and sides of the pan. Serve the capon carved, with the prunes and pan gravy.

Yield: About 10 servings. *Each serving provides: 355 cal, 34 g pro, 4 g sat fat, 11 g unsat fat, 66 mg chol, 265 mg sodium.*

Roast Chicken with Sweet Pepper Chutney

The chutney adds a zesty, piquant flavor and may be made ahead of time and stored in the refrigerator for up to 2 weeks.

1 broiler-fryer, about 3 pounds	1 large red bell pepper, seeded and cut into chunks (about 1 ¼ cups)
2 cloves garlic, peeled and crushed	½ teaspoon red pepper flakes
herbal seasoning and freshly grated pepper to taste	¼ teaspoon ground cloves
1 tablespoon chicken fat or olive oil	½ cup raisins
1 medium yellow onion, sliced (about 1 cup)	1 cup whole peeled tomatoes, drained
	2 tablespoons honey
	2 tablespoons lemon juice
	1 teaspoon grated lemon rind

Preheat oven to 450°F.

Rub the chicken inside and out with the garlic and the seasonings. Arrange the chicken on a rack in a shallow baking pan. Roast for 10 minutes. Reduce the oven temperature to 350°F. Roast for 30 minutes, basting with pan juices.

(continued)

Meanwhile, prepare the chutney.

In a skillet or heavy-bottom saucepan, combine the oil, onion, grated pepper, pepper flakes, and cloves. Cook over medium heat, stirring occasionally until the onions are transparent and the bell pepper is wilted. Add the raisins, tomatoes, honey, lemon juice, and rind. Simmer, uncovered, for about 10 minutes. Remove from the heat and allow to cool.

Serve the chicken either warm or cool, accompanied with the chutney at room temperature.

Yield: 4 servings. *Each serving provides: 150 cal, 25 g pro, 1.5 g sat fat, 2.7 g unsat fat, 66 mg chol.*

Roast Chicken with Rosemary and Garlic

The marvelous aroma of rosemary and garlic piques the appetite. I like to serve this flavorful chicken with a big tossed salad and julienned carrots steamed with currants.

1 *broiler fryer, 3 to 3½ pounds* *vegetable seasoner and* *pepper to taste*	2 *cloves garlic, unpeeled*
2 *sprigs fresh rosemary or ½* *teaspoon dried*	1 *onion, peeled* ¾ *cup water*

Preheat the oven to 425°F.

Sprinkle the chicken inside and out with the seasonings, then stuff it with the garlic and the rosemary.

Place the chicken on its side in a shallow roaster. Scatter the onion, neck, and gizzards around the chicken. Roast for 15 minutes, then turn the chicken on the other side and continue roasting, basting often for another 15 minutes. Then turn the chicken on its back and continue roasting and basting for 15 minutes.

Pour off the fat from the roasting pan. Add the water, and return the the oven. Roast 10 minutes longer, basting frequently. Remove from the oven and let stand 10 minutes before carving. Serve with the pan liquid.

Yield: 4 servings. *Each serving provides: 150 cal, 25 g pro, 1.5 g sat fat, 2.7 g unsat fat, 66 mg chol.*

3

EXOTIC CHICKEN BREASTS

The breast is especially delectable to lovers of the white meat. It is certainly the most versatile portion of the chicken's anatomy. It can be deboned and stuffed with nuts, seeds, fruits, grains, or vegetables. It can be spread with almond butter, peanut butter, cashew butter, or tahini, but not with dairy butter, which is a saturated fat. Nut butters provide healthier polyunsaturated fats.

Fat of some kind is usually added to chicken breasts because they tend to be dry. Many chefs remove the skin because it is fatty, then add another fat. I prefer to use the fat that is indigenous to the source. I leave the skin on. The fat in the chicken skin not only makes for a deliciously moist and flavorful chicken dish but also one that is much kinder to your heart. The fat in chicken skin is mainly monounsaturated, the kind that tends to lower harmful cholesterol levels. It is not necessary to eat the skin. Just cook with it and limit the addition of other fats.

In recipes that call for cutting up the breast, however, it may be necessary to remove the skin along with the bones. In that case, reserve both the skin and bones to make a tasty stock.

Chicken with Linguine

Savory, satisfying, ready in no time, and high in energetic complex carbohydrates. The added vegetables contribute vitamin B's, carotene, and important antioxidants.

2 whole chicken breasts
2 tablespoons soy sauce
2 tablespoons dry sherry
2 teaspoons cornstarch or
    potato starch
1 8-ounce package linguine,
    cooked
2 tablespoons olive oil or
    chicken fat
1 cup sliced mushrooms

1 cup pea pods or 1 cup
    mung bean sprouts
2 green onions, cut into
    2-inch pieces
1 red pepper, thinly sliced
½ cup chicken broth or
    ½ cup water mixed with
    ½ teaspoon
    chicken-flavored bouillon

On a cutting board or double thickness of wax paper, cut each chicken breast in half. Place the pieces skin side up. Work with one half at a time. Using the tip of a sharp knife, start close to the large end of the rib and remove the bones. Slide the skin off. Reserve both skin and bones for stock.

Slice across the width of each half into ½-inch slices.

In a bowl, combine the sliced chicken, soy sauce, sherry, and cornstarch or potato starch.

In a large skillet or wok, heat the oil or chicken fat. Add the mushrooms, pea pods or mung bean sprouts, green onions, and red pepper. Stir quickly until just tender, about 3 minutes. With a slotted spoon, remove the vegetables to a bowl. In the drippings remaining

(continued)

in the skillet or wok, cook the chicken mixture, stirring frequently until the chicken is tender, about 3 minutes. Return the vegetables to the skillet or wok. Add the chicken broth or water and bouillon. Heat to boiling, stirring to loosen the flavorful brown bits from the bottom of the skillet. Add the cooked linguine. Heat the mixture through. Toss to mix well.

Yield: 6 servings. *Each serving provides: 199 cal, 12.7 g pro, 2.3 g sat fat, 6.2 g unsat fat, 74 mg chol.*

Chicken au Poivre

Peps up the palate and the conversation. The vegetables round out the nutritional power and contribute beneficial fiber.

4 *large whole chicken breasts, boned and split*
2 *teaspoons coarsely ground black pepper*
1 *teaspoon herbal seasoning*
2 *tablespoons olive oil*
2 *tablespoons chicken fat*
1 *cup thinly sliced onions*
1 *cup thinly sliced carrots*
1 *clove garlic, crushed*
2 *tablespoons whole wheat flour*

½ *teaspoon dried thyme*
1 *bay leaf*
3 *tablespoons finely chopped fresh parsley*
½ *cup coarsely chopped celery*
½ *cup finely chopped leeks or scallions*
1 *cup dry vermouth*
1 *cup chicken broth*
1 *tablespoon prepared mustard, preferably Dijon*
1 *tablespoon chopped chives*

26

Sprinkle the chicken pieces with the pepper and herbal seasoning.

Heat the oil and chicken fat in a large skillet. Add the onions, carrots, and garlic and cook, stirring, about 10 minutes. Do not allow it to brown. Sprinkle with the flour, and stir to blend. Arrange the chicken pieces, boned-side down in the skillet and sprinkle with the thyme, bay leaf, parsley, celery, and leeks or scallions. Cover closely and cook for 5 minutes.

Add the vermouth and broth, and cover. Simmer for 20 minutes.

Remove the chicken pieces to a platter and keep warm. Spoon and scrape the sauce into the container of a food processor or blender and blend to a fine purée. Return the sauce to a saucepan and gently heat. Add the mustard, stirring, and remove from the heat. Sprinkle with the chives, and pour the sauce over the chicken. Serve hot.

Yield: 8 servings. *Each serving provides: 203.5 cal, 27 g pro, 3 g sat fat, 8 g unsat fat, 74 mg chol.*

Chicken Almond Delight

The intriguing scent and taste of almonds bring a subtle elegance to this very popular dish.

2 chicken breasts, split and boned
4 tablespoons chunky almond butter
½ teaspoon dried thyme
1 cup bread crumbs made from toasted whole wheat pita

2 tablespoons olive oil
1 tablespoon chicken fat
1 clove garlic
½ cup sherry

Pound the breasts flat and spread the almond butter on each. Combine the pita crumbs and thyme. Sprinkle this mixture over the chicken. In a large skillet, heat the oil and chicken fat and sauté the garlic briefly.

Roll up each chicken breast, and anchor with toothpicks. Place them in the skillet, and sauté for 1 minute. Place in a baking dish sprayed with nonstick spray, and bake at 350°F. for 20 minutes. Pour the sherry in the sauté pan, heat, and pour over the chicken breasts.

Yield: 4 servings. *Each serving provides: 381 cal, 24 g pro, 3.8 g sat fat, 16 g unsat fat, 74 mg chol.*

Variation 1: Substitute cashew or peanut butter for the almond butter.

Variation 2: For those who are allergic to wheat, substitute crushed rice cakes for the whole wheat pita.

Chicken with Pine Nuts

Lightly roasted pine nuts bring a lovely sensuous flavor to this easily prepared, delightful dish. Pine nuts are a good source of vitamin B complex, vitamin A, and many minerals, and are low in fat. They are expensive, but once in a while they're worth it.

1 tablespoon olive oil
1 tablespoon chicken fat
2 whole chicken breasts,
    deboned and cut in
    2-inch pieces

6 scallions, sliced
2 cloves garlic, minced
2 tomatoes, skinned and
    chopped
½ cup pine nuts, lightly roasted

In a large skillet, heat the oil and chicken fat. Over medium heat, cook the chicken until lightly browned. Add the scallions and garlic and cook another minute. Add the tomatoes. Cook for 15 to 20 minutes, or until the chicken is tender and thoroughly cooked. Sprinkle with the pine nuts.

Yield: 4 servings. *Each portion provides: 242 cal, 24 g pro, 2.5 g sat fat, 7 g unsat fat, 74 mg chol.*

Breast of Chicken Cock-a-doodle-doo

So called because of the way it remains moist and tender and puffs up with pride. Serve with sweet potato puff and cranberry chutney.

2 whole chicken breasts, boned and divided in halves
¼ cup whole wheat flour
3 tablespoons sesame seeds (optional)
1 tablespoon olive or canola oil
1 tablespoon chicken fat

Use the skin and bones to make a flavorful stock, which will be used in the gravy.

Dust the breasts lightly with the flour mixed with the sesame seeds.

Heat the oil and chicken fat together in a heavy skillet. Place the chicken pieces in the hot fat. Shake the pan constantly so the floury crusts do not brown. Cover and cook over very low heat for 10 to 15 minutes, depending on the thickness of the chicken, turning the meat occasionally.

Remove the pan from the heat and allow to stand, covered, about 10 minutes more. The breast will puff up and be unbelievably moist and tender. Remove the chicken from the pan and keep warm.

To make the gravy: Pour off and reserve the fat from the pan. In a saucepan heat 2 tablespoons of the fat and 2 tablespoons of the whole wheat flour. Slowly stir in the remaining pan juices and enough of the reserved stock to make 2 cups. Cook and stir the gravy until smooth, and simmer for 5 minutes.

Yield: 4 servings. *Each serving provides: 209 cal, 23 g pro, 1.2 g sat fat, 6.2 g unsat fat, 74 mg chol.*

Raisin and Rum Chicken in Creamy Almond Sauce

A poem for the palate—a sure winner. Even the picky eaters lick the platter clean. Serve with steamed brown rice, baked potatoes, or mammaligge (cornmeal mush) to soak up every bit of the delicious sauce.

3 tablespoons raisins
3 tablespoons rum
4 whole chicken breasts, halved and boned
¼ teaspoon each ginger, dry mustard, and thyme
¼ teaspoon pepper
¾ cup defatted, low-sodium chicken broth
¼ cup almonds, toasted
½ cup apple juice
½ teaspoon grated orange rind
2 tablespoons chopped almonds, toasted

In a small bowl, soak the raisins in the rum.

Heat a large, heavy skillet. Remove all visible fat from the chicken breasts and render the fat in the heated skillet. If there is more than 1 tablespoon, remove it and reserve for another use. Add the chicken to the skillet; sprinkle with the herbs and pepper. Cook over medium heat, turning often for about 10 minutes or until the flesh is firm. Remove to a plate and keep warm.

Add the broth to the skillet and bring to a boil. In a blender or food processor, blend the almonds, apple juice, and orange rind.

Add the almond mixture to the skillet, stirring constantly. Simmer for 3 minutes, then stir in the rum and raisins. Taste-check for seasoning.

(continued)

Reheat the cutlets gently in the hot sauce. Arrange in a heated serving dish, and spoon the sauce over all. Sprinkle with the chopped almonds.

Yield: 8 servings. *Each serving provides: 325 cal, 17.9 g pro, 2.8 g sat fat, 7.6 g unsat fat, 71 mg chol, 70 mg sodium.*

4

TASTY WAYS WITH CHICKEN PARTS

In our house, the children go for the drumstick; their parents go for a nice, plump thigh. For our family and for entertaining, I find that when I serve a chorus line of beautiful legs, no one is denied his or her favorite part, and everybody feels like dancing.

Chicken with 30 Cloves of Garlic

This is based on a very old recipe that called for 40 cloves of garlic. I ran out of cloves and courage when I got to 30-something. But don't be intimidated. Garlic has so many health benefits, some proven, some reputed. In Russia it is used like we use antibiotics. Eleanor Roosevelt claimed that it helped her memory. It has been shown to tame high blood pressure and lower cholesterol, and a recent survey reveals that garlic eaters have more immunity against the development of cancer. How nice to get all those benefits at one meal!

As for the taste, you'll find that the long cooking has given the garlic a delicious, creamy quality and tamed its pungency. Spread it on hot toast for a treat that warrants a standing ovation.

6 *chicken legs with thighs, washed and thoroughly dried*

30 *cloves garlic, peeled and left whole*

3 *stalks celery, washed and sliced*

½ *cup chicken broth*

½ *teaspoon dried thyme*

½ *teaspoon freshly grated ginger root or ¼ teaspoon dried*

¼ *teaspoon freshly ground pepper*

½ *teaspoon paprika*

1 *teaspoon herbal seasoning*

Preheat the oven to 350°F.

Heat a heavy casserole with a tight-fitting lid. Coat the bottom with nonstick baking spray. Place the chicken in the casserole and brown the chicken about 5 minutes on each side. Add the garlic and the celery, then the chicken broth. Add the thyme, ginger root, pepper, paprika, and herbal seasoning.

Cover the casserole tightly and bake for 1½ hours.

Yield: 6 servings. *Each drumstick provides: 100 cal, 16 g pro, 1.5 g sat fat, 3.9 g unsat fat, 70 mg chol, 248 mg sodium.*

Each thigh provides: 142 cal, 16 g pro, 2 g sat fat, 3.9 g unsat fat, 70 mg chol, 248 mg sodium.

Aunt Betty's Luscious Chicken with Mushrooms and Rice

Serve with a crisp green salad and you have a complete meal—delicious, high in fiber, and rich in cholesterol-reducing nutrients.

2 *cups water or chicken broth*	½ *teaspoon crushed, dried thyme*
1 *tablespoon olive, peanut, or canola oil*	½ *teaspoon paprika*
4 *drumsticks and 4 thighs, washed and dried*	¼ *teaspoon dry mustard (optional)*
1 *cup chopped onions*	¼ *teaspoon ground pepper*
1 *cup mushrooms, cleaned and sliced*	1 *cup brown rice, parboiled for 20 minutes*
1 *clove garlic, minced*	1 *can (1 pound) tomatoes*
¼ *teaspoon cayenne pepper*	1 *large green pepper, sliced*

Heat the oil in a heavy skillet. Brown the chicken. Add the onions, mushrooms, garlic, and cayenne pepper. Lightly sauté until the onions are golden—about 3 minutes.

Add the thyme, paprika, mustard, ground pepper, rice, tomatoes, and 2 cups of water or chicken broth. Bring to a boil, then reduce heat and cover. Simmer 20 minutes. Add the sliced pepper and cook, covered, for 10 minutes longer or until the chicken is tender and the peppers are still crisp-tender. Serve piping hot right from the skillet.

Yield: 8 servings. *Each drumstick provides: 212 cal, 17.8 g pro, 2 g sat fat, 5 g unsat fat, 75 mg chol, 73 mg sodium.*

Each thigh provides: 239 cal, 17.8 g pro, 2.5 g sat fat, 5.9 g unsat fat, 75 mg chol, 73 mg sodium.

Apricot and Almond Stuffed Thighs
with Tofu Mustard Sauce

8 chicken thighs
16 dried apricot halves
½ cup slivered almonds,
    toasted
1 teaspoon herbal seasoning
1 tablespoon minced onion
2 cups cooked brown rice

½ cup tofu
4 tablespoons fruit
    juice-sweetened apricot
    preserves
1 tablespoon prepared
    mustard (preferably salt
    free)

Preheat oven to 375°F.

Loosen the skin on the thighs. Place 2 apricot halves and 1 tablespoon of slivered almonds under the skin of each thigh. Sprinkle the thighs with the herbal seasoning and onion.

Place the thighs skin side up in a baking pan coated with nonstick cooking spray and bake for 40 to 45 minutes.

To make the sauce, combine the tofu, apricot preserves, and mustard, and heat but do not boil.

Serve the chicken on hot rice and pass the sauce.

Yield: 8 servings. *Each serving without sauce provides: 269 cal, 17.3 g pro, 3.3 g sat fat, 8 g unsat fat, 70 mg chol, 73 mg sodium.*

Each tablespoon of sauce provides: 30 cal, 0.7 g pro, no fat, no chol, 13 mg sodium.

Presto Crunchy Drumsticks

So easy to prepare and ready in a hurry. Great for spur-of-the-moment get-togethers and very popular with young people. Great with stewed tomatoes and fresh carrot sticks.

8 drumsticks
½ cup chicken stock

½ cup shredded wheat
minibiscuits, crushed
½ teaspoon cayenne pepper

Preheat oven to 375°F.

Dip the drumsticks in the chicken stock, then roll them in the crushed biscuits mixed with the cayenne pepper. Bake for 30 minutes or until golden brown and crunchy.

Yield: 8 servings. *Each serving provides: 101 cal, 13.7 g pro, 1.5 g sat fat, 3 g unsat fat, 75 mg chol, 88 mg sodium.*

Sesame Almond Sexy Legs

Sesame seeds were used by Egyptian sirens to enhance their sex appeal. Oat bran crunch provides cholesterol-lowering fiber. So think lovely thoughts while you indulge in this sensual dish.

¾ cup oat bran crunch,
   crushed
½ cup toasted sesame seeds
½ cup slivered almonds
1 tablespoon dried green
   onions

1 teaspoon dry mustard
½ teaspoon parsley flakes
½ teaspoon dried thyme
8 whole chicken legs
   (drumsticks and thighs)
1 cup pineapple juice

Preheat oven to 350°F.

Combine all the ingredients except the chicken and the pineapple juice. Dip the chicken in the pineapple juice, then coat with the crumb mixture. Place the chicken in a baking dish coated with non-stick cooking spray. Sprinkle with any remaining crumbs. Bake 45 minutes or until the chicken is tender.

Yield: Servings for 8 hearty eaters. *Each leg provides: 219 cal, 30 g pro, 1.4 g sat fat, 6 g unsat fat, 150 mg chol, 75 mg sodium.*

Stuffed Broiled Chicken Legs Rosemary

Simply sensational—a great party dish. Serve with cranberry chutney and sweet potato, apple, and granola casserole.

8 whole chicken legs
1½ teaspoons sodium-free
   herbal seasoner
   freshly ground pepper
2 tablespoons chicken fat or
   canola oil

¼ cup lemon or lime juice
2 teaspoons dried rosemary
2 teaspoons prepared mustard
   garnish: parsley and 1
   orange, sectioned

Carefully pull the skin of the thigh away from the meat. Sprinkle the flesh with herbal seasoner and pepper.

Blend together the chicken fat or oil with the lemon or lime juice, rosemary, and mustard. Spread about 2 teaspoons of this mixture under the skin of each thigh.

Place the chicken pieces, skin side down, in a broiling pan coated with nonstick cooking spray. Broil about 6 inches from the heat source for about 14 minutes, or until brown. Turn and broil the other side for another 14 minutes.

To serve, spread any remaining rosemary mixture on the chicken, place on a serving platter, pour the pan juices over the chicken, and garnish the platter with parsley and orange sections.

Yield: 8 servings. *Each serving provides: 200 cal, 24 g pro, 2 g sat fat, 3.04 g unsat fat, 150 mg chol, 85 mg sodium.*

5

WINNING WAYS WITH WINGS

Learn to go creative with wings and you'll win the battle of the budget. Wings can precede the meal as an appetizer or make the meal as a substantial entrée. There are approximately 9 wings in a pound. A plain wing provides 82 calories, almost 9 grams of protein, 28 mg of cholesterol, and 27 mg of sodium.

Sesame Chicken Wing Appetizers

Delectable succulence that adds pizzazz to your party. Make them ahead, then reheat in the microwave.

12 chicken wings, disjointed
    and tips removed
1 tablespoon olive, canola, or
    peanut oil
2 cloves garlic, crushed
2 slices fresh ginger root cut
    into very fine shreds
2 tablespoons Tamari soy
    sauce
2 tablespoons dry sherry

2 teaspoons Old Bay
    seasoning or herbal
    seasoner (optional)
¼ teaspoon freshly ground
    pepper
1 tablespoon toasted sesame
    seeds
2 tablespoons chopped green
    onions, including the
    green part

In a wok or skillet, heat the oil and add the garlic and ginger root. Stir briefly, then add the chicken wings. Cook, stirring, until lightly browned, about 3 minutes. Add the soy sauce and sherry and cook, stirring, about 30 seconds longer.

Cover and simmer about 10 minutes. Uncover, turn the heat to high, and continue cooking, stirring, until the liquid is almost evaporated and the chicken pieces are glazed.

Remove from the heat and add the seasoning or seasoner and pepper. Toss. Just before serving, toss in the sesame seeds and onions.

Yield: 12 appetizer servings. *Each serving provides: 95 cal, 8.7 g pro. 1.2 g sat fat, 3.1 g unsat fat, 28 mg chol, 197 mg sodium.*

Crockpot Winning Wings
in Chinese Sweet and Sour Sauce

A great no-fuss, do-ahead dish for a summer party, or for taking a winning covered dish, or to keep the buffet hot and spicy. The peanut butter adds an interesting Thailand flavor but can be omitted without changing the sweet and sour concept.

16 *chicken wings*
4 *tablespoons wine or balsamic vinegar*
1 *cup fruit juice-sweetened apricot conserves*
2 *tablespoons peanut butter (optional)*

1 *cup ketchup (see recipe for salt free ketchup)*
4 *tablespoons prepared horseradish*
1 *cup finely chopped sweet onion*
1 *teaspoon hot sauce (optional)*

Pat the chicken wings dry and place them in the Crockpot. In a bowl, mix together the remaining ingredients. Taste-check for a good balance of sweet and sour.

Pour the sauce over the wings. Cover the Crockpot and cook on low until the chicken is tender, usually 4 hours.

Yield: 16 flavorful wings. *Each wing provides: 160 cal, 8.8 g pro, 1 g sat fat, 7 g unsat fat, 28 mg chol, 220 mg sodium.*

Salt-Free Ketchup

4 cups fresh or canned, unsalted tomatoes
¾ cup tomato paste (unsalted)
1 cup chopped onions
1 small green pepper, cut into small cubes
2 tablespoons honey
1 bay leaf
¼ teaspoon each ground cloves, ground allspice, ground mace, dry mustard, and freshly ground black pepper
⅛ teaspoon cinnamon
1 teaspoon minced garlic
¼ cup malt or apple cider vinegar

In a saucepan, combine the tomatoes, tomato paste, onions, and green pepper. Bring to a boil and simmer for 30 minutes.

Put this mixture through a food mill, food processor, or blender and process thoroughly.

Return the blended sauce to the saucepan and add the remaining ingredients. Bring to a boil, then simmer, stirring frequently for about 10 minutes.

Yield: About 5 cups. *Each tablespoon provides: 8 cal, no fat, no chol, 2 mg sodium.*

Winged Victory
with Pineapple and Sweet Potatoes

½ cup whole wheat flour
¼ cup oat bran
1 teaspoon Old Bay seasoning or any good herbal seasoner
¼ teaspoon freshly ground pepper
16 chicken wings
½ cup chicken broth
1 tablespoon olive or canola oil or chicken fat

3 medium-size sweet potatoes or yams, steamed and peeled
1 (1-pound) can unsweetened pineapple chunks; reserve syrup
1 teaspoon Tamari soy sauce
3 tablespoons fruit juice-sweetened orange marmalade

In a clean paper bag, combine the flour, oat bran, seasoning or seasoner, and pepper. Dip the wings in the chicken broth, then shake with the flour mixture in the bag to coat.

Heat the oil or chicken fat in a baking dish in a 425°F oven. Arrange the wings in the pan and brown on each side (about 10 minutes on each side).

Remove the pan from the oven and intersperse the yams or sweet potatoes and pineapple chunks around the wings.

Combine the reserved pineapple juice, soy sauce, and marmalade, and spoon over all. Return to the oven and bake for another 20 minutes.

Yield: 8 servings. *Each serving provides: 234 cal, 18 g pro, 3.2 g sat fat, 4.5 g unsat fat, 56 mg chol, 115 mg sodium.*

Apples on the Wings

A real winner in the low-calorie, low-fat department. Apples are a rich source of pectin, which has been shown to escort the harmful factor of cholesterol out of the body. Ambrosia rice pudding makes a delicious accompaniment.

16 chicken wings, washed and dried
2 large apples, scrubbed, unpeeled, sliced
½ teaspoon ground cinnamon
1 teaspoon lemon juice
1 teaspoon honey
1 cup apple juice or apple cider
½ teaspoon Old Bay seasoning or a good herbal seasoner
¼ teaspoon freshly ground pepper

Arrange the wings in a heatproof casserole in a single layer. Combine the apples, cinnamon, lemon juice, and honey. Place the apple mixture over the wings. Combine the apple juice and seasonings and pour over all. Cover the casserole and bake in a 350°F oven for about 50 minutes, or until the wings are tender.

Yield: 16 wings. *Each wing provides: 100 cal, 8.8 g pro, 1.5 g sat fat, 3 g unsat fat, 28 mg chol, 28 mg sodium.*

Ambrosia Rice Pudding

1 can (20 ounces) pineapple
   chunks in juice
2 cups cooked brown rice
2 teaspoons grated orange
   rind
2 navel oranges, peeled and
   sectioned

1 banana, thinly sliced
½ cup fresh blueberries or
   sliced strawberries
2 tablespoons flaked coconut
   (unsweetened)

Drain the pineapple juice into a medium-size saucepan. Reserve the chunks. Bring the juice to a boil and stir in the rice. Remove from the heat, cover, and let cool.

Combine the pineapple, orange rind and orange sections, banana, berries, coconut, and rice in a glass bowl. Refrigerate for several hours.

Yield: 10 servings. *Each serving provides: 111 calories, 1 g pro, 1 g fat, no chol, 3 mg sodium.*

6

HEARTY, HEALING CHICKEN SOUPS

Prepare a good, hearty, flavorful soup and you've got it made. Soup warms the bones, cheers the heart, and is the oldest-known remedy for a cold.

There's no better vehicle than soup for enriching your body with important nutrients, for lifting your spirits, and for making recalcitrant eaters healthy when they're not looking.

Chicken soup—Jewish soul food and psychological medicine—can be hot, filling, cheering, satisfying, and custom-made. It can provide trace minerals, vitamins, and fiber and make you feel full and satisfied on very few calories.

You're getting a lot more out of that bowl of soup than a tantalizing aroma and a great blend of flavors. "Soup is the ideal replacement fluid," says Dr. George E. Burch in the February 1976 *American Heart Journal.* "Because vegetables, grains, and meats release their goodness into the fluid in which they are steeped, soup contains everything one finds in plant and animal tissues."

Almost all soups call for chicken broth or stock. Make a big pot of good, hearty chicken broth, cool and store jars of it in the freezer, or cool it and pour into ice cube trays. When the cubes are frozen solid, store them in a plastic bag tightly secured with a twistem or rubber band. Store in the freezer and use frequently to enrich soups or stews, to flavor cooked rice, or to replace fat in a stir-fry. It's liquid gold and better than money in the bank.

Basic Poultry Stock

The addition of an acid such as vinegar helps to release the calcium from the bones, thus enriching the broth. The veal bones enrich the flavor and give this broth more gusto.

1 chicken, duck, or turkey
carcass, broken apart (can
be cooked or uncooked)
giblets, gizzards, wings,
and necks (no liver)
chicken feet (if you can find
them) dipped in boiling
water and outer skin
removed
1 pound veal bones, chopped
into 2-inch pieces
3 quarts cold water, or to cover
1 large onion—skin, too—
stuck with 2 cloves
1 carrot, quartered
3 stalks celery, including
leaves, cut up

2 parsnips, pealed and sliced
1 parsley root, pealed and
sliced (optional)
3 to 4 leeks, cleaned and cut
into ½-inch pieces
2 bay leaves
½ teaspoon dried thyme
¼ teaspoon freshly grated
nutmeg
6 peppercorns
6 sprigs parsley
3 sprigs fresh dill
1 teaspoon herbed or cider
vinegar
1 clove garlic, halved
⅛ teaspoon poultry seasoning

In an 8-quart soup pot, combine the carcass, chicken parts, veal bones, and water. Bring to a boil, reduce the heat, and skim off any scum that has come to the surface.

Add the remaining ingredients and simmer for 3 to 4 hours, uncovered.

Strain the stock through a fine sieve. Cool quickly by placing the pot in a sink half filled with very cold water or over ice cubes. When cold, remove all the surface fat. Pour the broth into ice cube trays or pint jars and freeze.

Yield: About 6 cups. *One cup provides: 39 cal, 3.36 g pro, 0.48 g fat, no chol, 600 mg sodium.*

Microwave Method
The microwave does a good job of making stock in a hurry. Make it in 2 batches. Use a large casserole-type dish. Cover tightly and microcook on high for about 20 minutes, stirring midway. Let stand for another 20 minutes, then strain.

Chicken Stock and a Hearty Soup

1 medium stewing chicken,
    cut into pieces
    chicken giblets (not the liver)
    water to cover
1 large onion, including the
    skin
2 carrots, cut in quarters

¼ cup lemon juice
¼ teaspoon each of freshly
    ground pepper, paprika,
    basil, tarragon, and ginger
½ cup chopped parsley
2 stalks celery, including
    leaves, sliced

Wash the chicken and place in a deep pot. Cover with the water. Bring to a boil and skim. Add the remaining ingredients. Cover. Return to a boil, then lower the heat and simmer for 2 hours. Let the chicken cool in the soup; then skin the chicken, bone it, and refrigerate for another dish. Or strain, reserving the chicken and vegetables. Now you have several options: If you're serving the broth as broth, add some cooked brown rice, barley, or noodles and some chopped-up chicken and giblets.

Yield: About 10 servings. *Each serving provides: 39 cal, 3 g pro, 0.48 g fat, no chol, 130 mg sodium.*

Variation: Or you can make a very special eggnog that my mom always served to us when we had the sniffles or were convalescing from childhood diseases or the grippe (now called the flu). You feel stronger as you sip it.

In a soup bowl or in a food processor, beat an egg till frothy. Continue to beat as you slowly add a cup of hot broth. For adults, top with garlicky croutons. (If there is any danger of salmonella in your area, omit the egg.)

Chicken Egg Drop Soup

For extra crunch, fiber, calcium, and beta-carotene, stir in a cup of shredded romaine or escarole lettuce just before serving.

6 cups chicken broth	1 teaspoon soy sauce
2 tablespoons chopped parsley	2 eggs

In a 3-quart saucepan over medium-high heat, heat the broth and the soy sauce to boiling.

Meanwhile, in a small bowl, beat the eggs slightly. Slowly, with a fork, stir the eggs into the boiling soup, and stir until the eggs separate into shreds. Garnish with parsley.

Yield: 6 servings. *Each serving provides: 45 cal, 5.5 g pro, 3.4 g sat fat, 1.8 g unsat fat, 88 mg chol, 640 mg sodium.*

Mushroom, Barley, and Bean Chicken Soup

Practically a meal in a dish. The barley gives this soup a hearty, creamy, chewy texture that makes you think it must be fattening. Not so. It actually has less fat and more iron than brown rice. You can enjoy a half cup of cooked barley—with all its calcium, potassium, and niacin—at a cost of only 52 calories. Dried mushrooms add an incomparable flavor to this soup as well as the antistress vitamin pantothenate, niacin, riboflavin, copper, and selenium, which is a valuable antiaging antioxidant.

½ cup large dry lima beans
¼ cup mung beans or brown
   lentils
¼ cup coarse barley
2 quarts water or stock,
   including the giblets (but
   not the liver)
1 3-pound chicken, cut up
3 marrow bones
2 cloves garlic
2 tablespoons dried
   mushrooms
1 large onion, diced

2 ribs celery with leaves,
   sliced
1 cup chopped carrots
1 turnip or ½ rutabaga,
   chopped
½ cup chopped fresh parsley
   or 2 tablespoons dried
3 sprigs of fresh dill or 1
   teaspoon dried
1½ teaspoons Tamari soy sauce

Wash the beans and barley and place in a large soup kettle with the water or stock, chicken, and marrow bones rubbed with the garlic. Bring to a boil and skim. Add the remaining ingredients, cover, and allow to simmer gently (make the pot smile) for about 2 hours or until the beans are soft. Remove the chicken and serve separately.

Yield: 10 servings. *Each serving provides: 51 cal, 2.3 g pro, 1.9 g unsat fat, about 400 mg sodium.*

Note: If your family doesn't particularly relish boiled chicken, remove the chicken after 45 minutes of cooking in the soup. Put the chicken in a baking dish; rub with garlic; and sprinkle with lemon juice, paprika, ginger, thyme, dry mustard, and a little bit of sage. Roast in a preheated 350°F oven, uncovered, until delicately browned.

Hawaiian Luau Bisque

It may sound strange, but it's simply wonderful!

6 *cups chicken stock*
3 *carrots, scrubbed, cut in chunks and slightly steamed, or microwaved, covered, on high for 3 minutes*

⅓ *cup peanut butter*
½ *cup soft tofu*
3 *tablespoons light rum*
¼ *cup unsweetened shredded coconut, shredded raw carrots, or flaked chicken*

In a large soup pot, heat the chicken stock. In a bowl or in the food processor, blend the carrots, peanut butter, and tofu. Blend this mixture into 1 cup of the hot stock, then add this mixture to the remainder of the stock, stirring constantly until smooth and creamy. Add

(continued)

the rum. Serve very hot with a topping of coconut, shredded carrots, or flaked chicken.

Yield: 10 servings. *Each serving provides: 92 cal, 4.5 g pro, 1 g sat fat, 3 g unsat fat, trace of chol, 651 mg sodium.*

Chicken Bouillabaisse

Much less expensive than the Mediterranean version but just as delicious!

3 *cups chicken broth or water*	2 *shallots or scallions, chopped*
3 *onions, chopped*	1 *can (1 pound) tomatoes, undrained*
1 *onion, studded with 4 cloves*	½ *teaspoon saffron threads (optional)*
1 *clove garlic, minced*	1 *teaspoon honey*
½ *cup chopped celery*	1⅓ *cups dry white wine*
4 *parsley sprigs, chopped*	6 *slices French bread or challah, toasted, and rubbed with garlic on both sides*
1 *tablespoon fresh thyme or 1 teaspoon dried*	
1 *broiler-fryer, about 3 pounds*	

In a large soup kettle, combine the chicken broth or water, onions (including the clove-studded one), garlic, celery, parsley, and thyme. Bring to a boil and simmer for 30 minutes.

Remove the skin and visible fat from the chicken. Cut into smallish pieces.

In a skillet, render the fat from the chicken skin. Remove the cracklings and reserve for another use. Sauté the shallots or scallions lightly in the same skillet. Remove from the skillet and reserve. Cut the chicken into small pieces and brown in the same skillet, turning once. Cook uncovered for about 10 minutes.

With a fork, break up the pieces of tomato and add to the chicken. Cook for 5 minutes. Add the chicken mixture to the soup kettle with the shallots or scallions, saffron, honey, and wine. Discard the clove-studded onion. Cook over low heat for about 1 hour or until the chicken is tender.

To serve, place a slice of toasted French bread or challah, rubbed on both sides with garlic, in each serving bowl. Spoon some chicken and soup over each.

Yield: 6 servings. *Each serving provides: 248 cal, 37 g pro, 2 g sat fat, 4 g unsat fat, 66 mg chol, 467 mg sodium.*

7

SAUTÉED, POACHED, AND GRILLED CHICKEN

Enjoy the smart alternative to deep-fat fried chicken. The crunchy, gusty, irresistible succulence of the reduced-calorie recipes in this chapter will take you from the Caribbean to Kentucky, New Orleans, and Tanzania, and in good health all the way.

Crunchy Chicken Cutlets:
A Romantic Dinner for Two

A smart alternative to costly veal cutlets, with added heart-healthy fiber. Serve with baked sweet potatoes and cranberry chutney.

1 chicken breast, boned, cut in half and skinned (reserve the skin and bones for stock or rendering)
1 egg
2 tablespoons water
pinch of cayenne pepper
2 tablespoons oat bran

2 tablespoons crushed shredded wheat or wheat germ
1 tablespoon olive, peanut, or canola oil
1 tablespoon chicken fat
juice of 1 lemon
2 tablespoons chopped parsley

Flatten the cutlets by pounding with a mallet or a heavy skillet until about ½-inch thick.

Beat the egg with the water and the cayenne pepper. On a piece of waxed paper, combine the oat bran and crushed shredded wheat or wheat germ.

Dip the cutlets into the egg mixture, then coat with the oat bran-wheat mixture.

In a large skillet, heat the oil and chicken fat. Add the chicken cutlets and sauté for about 3 minutes on each side, or until the meat is no longer pink all the way through. Test by cutting into them.

(continued)

Transfer to a serving platter and keep warm. Pour the lemon juice into the skillet and cook over high heat for about 1 minute, stirring constantly. Stir in the parsley. Pour the sauce over the chicken and serve.

Yield: 2 servings. *Each serving provides: 331 cal, 29 g pro, 2.58 g sat fat, 3.86 g unsat fat, 200 mg chol, 203 mg sodium.*

Chicken Sauté with Eggplant and Peanuts

Out of Africa with a zingy flavor. Great with brown rice or kasha.

1 *tablespoon olive, peanut, or canola oil*
1 *tablespoon chicken fat*
1 *chicken, about 3 pounds, cut into 8 pieces*
1 *large onion, diced*
3 *cloves garlic, minced*
2 *medium-size eggplants, cut into 1-inch cubes*
1 *tablespoon whole wheat flour*

1½ *cups chicken stock*
½ *cup dry white wine*
½ *cup shelled unsalted peanuts*
3 *bay leaves*
⅛ *teaspoon cayenne pepper*
½ *teaspoon dried thyme*
¼ *teaspoon dried sage*
¼ *teaspoon dried ginger*
¼ *teaspoon freshly ground pepper*

In a large skillet heat the oil and chicken fat. Add the chicken pieces. Brown on both sides. Add the onion, garlic, and eggplants. Sauté for 3 minutes. Dust with the flour. Add the chicken stock and wine. Bring to a boil, then reduce the heat to medium. Add the remaining ingredients. Cover the skillet and cook for about 45 minutes or until the chicken is tender.

Remove the chicken to a serving platter. Remove the bay leaves, Pour the sauce with the peanuts over the chicken and serve.

Yield: 6 servings. *Each serving provides: 196 cal, 20 g pro, 1 g sat fat, 2.2 g unsat fat, 85 mg chol, 329 mg sodium.*

Lime and Garlic Chicken

This low-calorie delight is always a favorite at our house. If you don't have chicken breasts on hand, substitute legs, drumsticks, or a cut-up broiler-fryer. Serve with a bulgur-sprouts pilaf (the recipe follows).

¼ cup lime juice
½ cup reduced-sodium soy
 sauce
½ teaspoon ground mustard
½ teaspoon ground pepper

1 tablespoon Worcestershire
 sauce
2 chicken breasts, halved,
 boned, and skinned

Mix together all the ingredients except the chicken. Pour the sauce over the chicken. Cover and marinate in the refrigerator for at least 30 minutes. Spray a skillet with nonstick cooking spray. Add the chicken and cook for 6 minutes on each side. Test for doneness. It should be opaque all the way through.

Yield: 4 servings. *Each serving provides: 130 cal, 25 g pro, 1.5 g fat, 75.5 mg chol, 489 mg sodium.*

Bulgur-Sprouts Pilaf with Almonds

A lovely marriage of flavors and textures. Almonds provide a touch of elegance as well as several B vitamins, calcium, iron, and magnesium. Bean sprouts provide a taste of spring, fantastic nutrients, and fiber. When paired with a grain like bulgur, they greatly enhance the quality of the protein.

1 cup bulgur
1 cup fresh mushrooms, sliced
1 tablespoon olive, peanut, or canola oil
3 cups vegetable or chicken broth
2 medium carrots, shredded

½ teaspoon vegetable seasoner
1½ cups mung bean or alfalfa sprouts
½ large green or red pepper, chopped
½ cup chopped almonds

In a large casserole, sauté the bulgur and mushrooms in the oil for 5 minutes or until lightly browned. Stir in the broth, carrots, and vegetable seasoner. Bring to a boil. Cover and place in a preheated 350°F oven for 20 minutes or until the broth is absorbed, stirring occasionally. Add the sprouts and pepper. Return to the oven for 5 more minutes, then add the almonds.

Yield: 6 servings. *Each serving provides: 163 cal, 7.2 g pro, 1 g sat fat, 11 g unsat fat, no chol, 417 mg sodium.*

Grilled Chicken Oregano

(low-sodium and very low in calories)

The Greeks called oregano "joy of the mountains." The lusty flavor of this dish, which is delicious either grilled over charcoal or broiled in the oven, will bring joy to your taste buds.

4 *chicken legs*
¼ *cup chopped onions*
¼ *cup lemon juice*
⅓ *cup low-sodium vegetable cocktail*
3 *cloves garlic, minced*
1 *teaspoon dried oregano or 1 tablespoon fresh*

½ *teaspoon freshly ground pepper*
1 *teaspoon herbal seasoner*
½ *teaspoon paprika*
2 *potatoes, scrubbed, unpeeled, sliced thin (optional)*
1 *cup mushrooms, washed and dried (optional)*

To prepare the chicken for either method, cut away all the visible fat and some of the fatty skin. Set aside. Place the legs in a baking dish sprayed with nonstick cooking spray. Cut 4 slits about ¼-inch deep in the meaty part of each leg.

In a small, heavy skillet, heat the reserved chicken fat and skin. Add the onions. Cook on medium high until the onions and skin are crisp. Watch them carefully—don't let the onions blacken. Remove the crisped onions and cracklings. Reserve the chicken fat that remains in the skillet—it will probably be less than a tablespoon, just enough to contribute an incomparable flavor.

Add the lemon juice, vegetable cocktail, garlic, oregano, pepper, herbal seasoner, and paprika to the skillet and heat until bubbly.

TO CHARCOAL-BROIL: With the skin side down, pour some of the lemon mixture over the chicken and grill about 5 inches from very hot coals. Turn and baste with the mixture frequently for about 40 minutes or until the juices run clear when the thighs are pierced and the meat is fork-tender. After 20 minutes into the grilling, surround the chicken with the sliced potatoes and the mushrooms if you're using them. Turn and baste them, too, with the lemon mixture.

TO BROIL IN THE OVEN: With the skin side up, pour some of the lemon mixture over the chicken and broil at 400°F about 6 inches from the heat source for about 20 minutes, basting 3 times. Add the potatoes and mushrooms. Turn and, basting the chicken and the vegetables 3 times, broil for about 20 minutes or until fork-tender.

Yield: 4 servings. *Each serving with potatoes and mushrooms provides: 271 cal, 29.6 g pro, 3.7 g sat fat, 4.2 g unsat fat, 76 mg chol, 92 mg sodium.*

Coolfont Broiled Chicken Breasts with Brown and Wild Rice and Zesty Tomato Sauce

We enjoy this dish, a nutritional powerhouse, at our favorite health retreat in West Virginia. Brown rice is the highest of all grains in the B vitamins. It also provides vitamin A, calcium, and iron and includes the cholesterol-lowering, fiber-rich rice bran. Wild rice, a grass, is richer in protein, minerals, and B vitamins than most grains.

The acidity of the tomato sauce helps the body to utilize the minerals more efficiently.

1 cup brown rice
½ cup wild rice
2 cups water
1 cup defatted chicken broth

3 boneless chicken breasts,
halved, skin on to seal in
the flavor and keep the
meat moist

In a saucepan, heat 2 cups of water and 1 cup of defatted chicken broth. Add the brown rice and the wild rice and cook for about 40 minutes or until the rice is tender.

Preheat the broiler to 400°F. Broil the chicken breasts about 6 inches below the heat source for about 4 minutes on each side, or until they are fork-tender. Remove the skin. Divide the rice mixture among 6 plates. Place a chicken breast on each plate and serve with a zesty tomato sauce.

ZESTY TOMATO SAUCE

1 cup canned plum tomatoes,
drained, diced
1 garlic clove, minced

1 tablespoon minced onion or
shallot
1 teaspoon dried basil or 1
tablespoon fresh

In a saucepan, combine all ingredients and simmer for 5 minutes. Serve hot.

Yield: 6 servings. *Each serving with rice and sauce provides: 307 cal, 36.7 g pro, 2 g sat fat, 3.7 g unsat fat, 77 mg chol, 262 mg sodium.*

Grilled Chicken with Herbs and Walnuts

A favorite of ours for outdoor grilling. The fantastic aroma of the chicken mingling with the herbs is so appetite-teasing the kids can hardly wait to bite into it.

2 broiler-fryers, about 2 pounds each
2 teaspoons dried basil or ½ cup fresh basil leaves
2 cloves garlic, minced
½ cup walnuts, chopped fine
½ teaspoon hot pepper sauce
¼ teaspoon freshly ground pepper
1 teaspoon olive or canola oil
1 tablespoon lemon juice
1 tablespoon white wine

Clean the chickens, then split them in halves. Cut off all the excess fat, loosen the skin, and remove any fat imbedded underneath.

In a small, heavy skillet, render the fat. Remove all but 1 tablespoon of rendered fat and reserve for another use.

Add the basil, garlic, walnuts, hot pepper sauce, and pepper to the fat in the skillet. Reserve 2 tablespoons of this mixture. Press the remaining mixture under the skin of the chickens, reaching as many areas as you can.

When the charcoal is white-hot, grill the chicken skin side up for about 15 minutes.

Add the oil, lemon juice, and wine to the reserved herb mixture. Brush some of this mixture on the underside of the chicken.

Turn the chicken and grill 15 minutes longer, brushing the undersides several times while it is cooking.

Yield: 4 servings. *Each serving provides: 378 cal, 50 g pro, 2.07 g sat fat, 4.14 g unsat fat, 148 mg chol, 133 mg sodium.*

Braised Chicken with Burgundy

2 broiler-fryers (about 2 to 2 ½ pounds each) cut in serving-size pieces
¼ cup whole wheat flour
⅔ cup Burgundy
½ cup chicken stock
1 can (8 ounces) sliced mushrooms; reserve the liquid

1 can (1 pound) small white onions, drained
2 tablespoons chopped parsley
½ teaspoon dried thyme
½ teaspoon dried marjoram
½ teaspoon freshly ground pepper
½ teaspoon herbal seasoner

Clean the chicken and remove all visible fat. Set aside.

In a heavy skillet, render the fat. Remove all but 2 tablespoons of fat. If you don't have 2 tablespoons of chicken fat, add olive or canola oil to make 2 tablespoons.

Brown the chicken pieces on all sides. Transfer the chicken to a baking dish.

Add the flour to the drippings in the skillet and blend well. Add the Burgundy, chicken stock, mushrooms, and liquid from the mushrooms. Cook, stirring constantly, until the mixture boils and thickens. Add the onions, thyme, marjoram, parsley, pepper, and herbal seasoner.

Yield: 4 servings. *Each serving provides: 290 cal, 52 g pro, 2.07 g sat fat, 4.14 g unsat fat, 66 g chol, 133 mg sodium.*

Poaching

Back in the seventeenth century, chicken on the table was a symbol of prosperity. It was good King Henry IV of France who said that everyone in his kingdom should have a chicken in his pot every Sunday.

Chicken cooked in a pot is poached. The pot liquor is good old chicken soup.

How does poaching differ from braising? In braising, the bird is browned in fat beforehand, then simmered in relatively little liquid in a covered pot.

In poaching, more liquid is used, and the liquid is plain water or stock. The art of successful poaching is regulating the temperature of the liquid throughout the cooking process. The bird should be immersed in cold water that is brought slowly to a boil. During the cooking period the liquid should be kept just below the boiling point to prevent the bird from drying out and becoming stringy.

When the chicken is done, skim off any surface fat. Put a slice of toast in each soup plate. For a really zingy taste that will knock your diners' socks off, rub the toast all over with garlic.

8

WONDERFULLY GOOD CHICKEN POT PIE

Chicken pot pie is practically the soul food of the Pennsylvania Dutch. And why not? It can be soul-satisfying, tummy-warming, and spirit-lifting. And so easy and quick to put together.

Every region and every country has its own version of chicken pot pie. The Pennsylvania Dutch version is made with some member of the pasta family. The British version calls for a pie crust enclosing the steaming aromatic chicken and vegetables.

If you have leftover cooked chicken, your pot pie is half made.

Pennsylvania Dutch Chicken Pot Pie

1 chicken (3½ to 4 pounds)
   cut into 8 serving pieces
water to cover
1 teaspoon herbal seasoning
¼ teaspoon freshly ground
   pepper

3 large potatoes, scrubbed,
   unpeeled, sliced about
   ½-inch thick
1 large onion, sliced
4 sprigs parsley
1 cup uncooked pot pie bows

In a heavy pot with a tight-fitting lid, simmer the chicken with the water, herbal seasoning, and pepper until the chicken is almost tender (about 25 minutes). Add the potatoes, onion, and parsley. Bring to a boil, then continue to simmer, covered, until the vegetables are not quite done, about 15 minutes. Drop the pot pie bows on top of the potatoes and onion. cover the pot again and simmer for about 20 minutes longer.

Serve in a heated tureen or casserole with the bows on top.

Yield: 6 hearty servings. *Each serving provides: 289 cal, 15 g pro, 2.7 g sat fat, 6.7 g unsat fat, 71 mg chol, 50 mg sodium.*

Chicken with Wheat and Oat Bran Dumplings

Follow the recipe for Pennsylvania Dutch chicken pot pie. Instead of topping it with pasta for the last 20 minutes of cooking, top it with these luscious dumplings and enjoy a high-fiber alternative.

1 cup whole wheat flour
¼ cup oat bran
2 teaspoons baking powder

2 tablespoons chopped fresh parsley
⅔ cup chicken broth

In a small bowl, combine the flour, oat bran, baking powder, and parsley. Gradually add the chicken broth, and stir to blend. Drop heaping tablespoons of dough into the simmering pot of soup or stew. Cover the pot and simmer for 15 to 20 minutes or until the dumplings are soft and mushy on the outside and breadlike on the inside.

Yield: About 8 large dumplings. *Each dumpling provides: 54 cal, 2 g pro, just a trace of fat, no chol, about 25 mg sodium.*

Chicken in Wine over Noodles

1 small chicken (about 2 to 2½ pounds), cut into serving pieces
¼ cup whole wheat flour
¼ cup finely chopped onions
1 garlic clove, crushed
¼ teaspoon rosemary
¼ teaspoon marjoram
2 cups low-sodium chicken broth

½ teaspoon freshly ground pepper
1 (1-pound can) tomatoes
1 bay leaf
1 carrot, sliced
1 stalk celery, sliced
1 cup mushrooms, sliced
¼ cup white wine
6 ounces egg noodles

Remove all visible fat and some of the skin from the chicken and render it in a heavy skillet. Remove all but 1 tablespoon of the fat and the chicken cracklings. Reserve for another use.

Dredge the chicken pieces with 2 tablespoons of the flour; sauté until golden. Remove the chicken from the pan. Add the onions to the pan and sauté until soft. Add the garlic, rosemary, and marjoram, and cook for a few minutes longer but do not allow it to brown. Blend in 2 tablespoons of flour. Gradually add the chicken broth and cook, stirring constantly, until thickened. Add the tomatoes, pepper, chicken, bay leaf, carrot, and celery. Simmer slowly for 15 minutes. Add the mushrooms and wine. Bring to a boil. Cover, reduce the heat, and simmer slowly for 30 minutes or until the chicken is tender. Remove the bay leaf.

Cook the noodles and drain. Place on a heated serving dish and top with the chicken. Pour the sauce over all.

Yield: 6 servings. *Each serving provides: 299 cal, 16 g pro, 2.7 g sat fat, 6.7 g unsat fat, 71 mg chol, 572 mg sodium.*

English-Style Chicken Pot Pie

In this recipe, the unusually flavorful, heart-healthy pie crust shares honors with the filling.

1 chicken, (about 3½ pounds), cut into 8 serving pieces
1 teaspoon herbal seasoning
½ teaspoon ground pepper
1 cup carrots, scraped and cut into thin rounds
1 cup chopped onions
½ cup chopped celery
1 clove garlic, minced
3 sprigs fresh parsley
¼ teaspoon dried thyme
1 bay leaf

3 tablespoons whole wheat flour
¾ cup dry, white wine
2 cups chicken or vegetable broth or water
⅛ teaspoon freshly ground nutmeg
1 tablespoon Worcestershire sauce
pie pastry (recipe follows)
1 egg yolk
1 tablespoon water

Place the chicken in a heavy casserole, skin side down. Sprinkle with the herbal seasoning and pepper. Cook, uncovered, till just golden brown on one side. Turn the pieces. Scatter the carrots, onions, celery, and garlic over the chicken pieces.

Add the parsley, thyme, bay leaf, and more pepper.

Sprinkle with flour. Stir until the pieces are coated. Add the wine and the broth or water. Bring to a boil. Stir and cover. Reduce the heat to simmer. Simmer for 30 minutes or until the chicken is tender.

Transfer the chicken to a shallow baking dish, preferably an oval dish about 14 x 8 x 2 inches. Scatter the onions on top.

(continued)

Skim off fat from the sauce in which the chicken cooked. Pour the sauce into a saucepan; add the nutmeg and Worcestershire sauce. Bring the sauce to a boil and pour it over the chicken mixture. Let cool.

Roll out the pastry large enough to more than fit the rim of the baking dish. Fit the pastry over the dish, pressing it tightly onto the rim and outer sides.

Whisk egg yolk with tablespoon of water to make a glaze. Brush the glaze over the pie crust.

Place the dish in an oven preheated to 400°F and bake for 30 minutes.

Pie Pastry

3 heaping tablespoons tahini
or sesame butter
1 cup whole wheat flour

1 teaspoon herbal seasoning
4 tablespoons ice water

In a food processor, combine the tahini or sesame butter, flour, and herbal seasoning.

Start processing and gradually add through the funnel only enough water to make a dough that holds together. Add as little water as possible.

Turn the dough out onto waxed paper and knead briefly. Roll out to fit the baking dish.

Yield: 6 servings. *Each serving provides: 339 cal, 18 g pro, 3.7 g sat fat, 8.7 g unsat fat, 71 mg chol, 572 mg sodium.*

Variation: Instead of the tahini or sesame butter crust, you can use a mashed potato crust. Cook 2 medium-size potatoes, mash, and add an egg and 2 tablespoons of chicken broth or water. Spoon evenly over the chicken mixture. Bake in a 350°F oven for 15 minutes.

9

CHICKEN WITH FRUIT

It's a wonderful marriage. The fruit brings moisture, flavor, fiber, and important vitamins and minerals to the marriage. The vitamin C in the fruit helps the body to utilize the iron in the chicken. The vitamin C also tenderizes the meat, reducing the cooking time.

Chicken or Turkey Cutlets
with a Delightful Kiwifruit Sauce

Easy to prepare, low-calorie, and nutrient-dense. Wonderful for instant meals. Prepare them when you have a few spare moments, store in the freezer, and you're ready for the hungry hordes.

1 egg white
1 tablespoon water
½ cup dry whole grain bread crumbs, oat bran, or a combination of these
1 teaspoon paprika

½ teaspoon freshly ground pepper
1 pound chicken or turkey breast cutlets, cut in slices ⅛- to ¼-inch thick

SAUCE

⅓ cup fruit juice-sweetened apricot preserves or orange marmalade

2 kiwifruit, pared and sliced
1½ teaspoons prepared horseradish

In a shallow bowl, beat the egg white with the water. Set aside. Combine bread crumbs, oat bran, or combination; the paprika; and the pepper on waxed paper. Dip the cutlets into the egg mixture, then into the crumb mixture. Arrange the breaded cutlets on a baking sheet lined with waxed paper. Place in the freezer for about 30 minutes, then transfer to a freezer bag. Return to the freezer until ready to bake.

When ready to serve, preheat the oven to 400°F. Spray a baking sheet with nonstick cooking spray. Arrange the cutlets on the baking sheet and bake for about 9 minutes for the ⅛-inch slices and for about

10 minutes for the ¼-inch slices or until the meat is no longer pink in the center.

TO MAKE THE SAUCE: Over medium-high heat, heat the apricot preserves in a small saucepan. Stir in the kiwifruit and horseradish. Heat until warm. Serve over cutlets.

TO MAKE THE SAUCE IN THE MICROWAVE: In a small bowl, microcook the marmalade or preserves, covered with waxed paper, for 60 seconds on high. Add the cut-up kiwifruit and the horseradish. Microcook for another 10 seconds or until the sauce is heated.

Yield: 4 servings. *Each serving with 2 tablespoons of sauce provides: 170 cal, 29 g pro, 1 g sat fat, 2.3 unsat fat, 66 mg chol, 60 mg sodium.*

Chicken with Prunes

Prunes, the wrinkled plums that have won a reputation as a "morning regular," contribute fiber, lots of immunity-building vitamin A, and a regular gold mine of magnesium, iron, and potassium.

1 3 ½- to 4-pound chicken,
   whole or cut up
2 teaspoons cumin
1 teaspoon Hungarian paprika
1 clove garlic, minced

½ teaspoon freshly ground
   pepper
1 cup seedless prunes
2 cups water
1 onion, sliced

Wipe the chicken dry with paper towels and place in a heavy casserole or roasting pan. Sprinkle with the cumin, paprika, garlic, and pepper. Allow to sit for 20 minutes so the spices can penetrate. Meanwhile, soak the prunes in the water.

Preheat the oven to 350°F.

Arrange onion slices over and around the chicken. Add the prunes with the soak water. Cover and cook for 1 hour or until the meat is tender and the juices run clear.

Yield: 4 servings. *Each serving provides: 235 cal, 28 g pro, 1 g sat fat, 2.3 g unsat fat, 70 mg chol, 57 mg sodium.*

Peachy Chicken Piquant
over Fluffy Brown Rice

Brown rice contains the cholesterol-lowering rice bran as well as the important B vitamins that help you keep your cool and is a good source of magnesium, the nutrient that puts a twinkle in your eye.

12 pieces of chicken
(drumsticks, thighs,
and/or breast halves)
½ teaspoon ground pepper
¾ cup low-sodium ketchup
1 can (16 ounces) sliced
peaches, drained; reserve
the juice
1 cup water

2 tablespoons reduced-sodium
Tamari soy sauce
1 large onion, sliced
1 large red or green pepper,
cut in squares
3 teaspoons arrowroot or
cornstarch
¼ cup water
3 cups hot cooked brown rice

Dry the chicken with paper towels and sprinkle with pepper. Place skin side up in a 2½-quart casserole sprayed with nonstick cooking spray.

Bake at 450°F for 20 minutes.

Combine the ketchup, peach syrup, soy sauce, and enough water to make 2 cups. Pour over the chicken. Top with the onion separated into rings.

Cover and bake 30 minutes longer. Add the pepper, peaches, and arrowroot or cornstarch dissolved in ¼ cup water. Cover and bake for 20 more minutes.

Serve with the sauce over hot brown rice.

Yield: 6 servings. *Each serving (2 pieces of chicken and ½ cup rice) provides: 382 cal, 33 g pro, 2 g sat fat, 4 g unsat fat, 70 mg chol, 130 mg sodium.*

Honolulu Chicken with Pineapple

Savor the spirit and flavor of Hawaii with this very popular quick-and-easy dish.

1 can (20 ounces) unsweetened pineapple chunks with juice
2 tablespoons reduced-sodium Tamari soy sauce
2 tablespoons lemon juice

1 tablespoon honey
½ teaspoon fresh ginger, minced
1 tablespoon minced onion
1 broiler chicken, cut into 8 parts

In a bowl, combine all the ingredients except the chicken.

Put the chicken in another deep bowl and pour the marinade over it. Refrigerate for 1 hour.

Place the chicken parts in a large baking pan. Pour marinade over the chicken and place in a preheated 350°F oven. Cover and bake for about 1 hour. Remove the cover for the last 15 minutes of baking.

Yield: 6 servings. *Each serving provides: 239 cal, 28 g pro, 1 g sat fat, 2.3 g unsat fat, 66 mg chol, 107 mg sodium.*

Roast Chicken or Turkey Breast
with Spicy Cherry Sauce

The breast or breasts are roasted with the skin on to keep the meat moist and flavorful, but the skin is removed before serving.

1 turkey breast or 3 chicken breasts (about 4 pounds)
1 can (16 ounces) pitted Bing cherries, drained; reserve the juice
1 tablespoon vinegar (preferably balsamic)
1 tablespoon honey
½ teaspoon cinnamon
⅛ teaspoon ground cloves
⅛ teaspoon ground nutmeg
¼ teaspoon ground ginger
2 tablespoons arrowroot or cornstarch
¼ cup cold water

Place the washed and dried breasts in a shallow roasting pan. Roast in a preheated 325°F oven for 1½ to 2 hours or until the meat is tender.

Meanwhile, combine in a small saucepan the cherry juice, vinegar, honey, and spices. Bring to a boil, then reduce the heat and cook for 10 minutes.

Mix the arrowroot or cornstarch with ¼ cup of cold water and add it to the hot liquid, stirring constantly until the sauce is thickened. Add the cherries and heat.

Remove the roasted breasts from the oven. Let them rest for about 10 minutes. Remove the skin and slice the meat. Spoon 2 tablespoons of hot cherry sauce over each serving.

Yield: 8 servings. *Each serving provides: 206 cal, 29 g pro, 1 g sat fat, 2.3 g unsat fat, 150 mg chol, 97 mg sodium.*

Chicken with Pineapple, Love, and Wheat Germ

Enjoy the slightly oriental flavor of this immensely popular dish. The wheat germ provides morale-boosting B vitamins and valuable fiber. Sesame seeds are high in vitamin E and were used by ancient Egyptian beauties to enhance their sex appeal.

2 large chicken breasts	1 clove garlic
2 tablespoons sesame seeds	1 cup canned pineapple
3 tablespoons wheat germ	chunks, drained
1 tablespoon chicken fat or	1 cup hot reduced-sodium
peanut oil	chicken broth
1 cup sliced mushrooms	2 tablespoons arrowroot or
¼ teaspoon freshly ground	cornstarch
pepper	2 cups hot cooked brown rice

Remove skin from the chicken breasts and reserve. Slice the chicken into bite-size chunks.

Render the chicken skin in a large, heavy skillet or wok. Remove all but 1 tablespoon of fat, or use the peanut oil instead.

Sauté the chicken chunks, sesame seeds, and wheat germ in the fat until the chicken turns white. Add the mushrooms, ground pepper, and garlic. Cook a few minutes longer over medium heat. Add the pineapple chunks.

In a small bowl, dissolve the arrowroot or cornstarch in a few tablespoons of the chicken broth before adding the remaining broth. Stir into the chicken mixture. Cook, stirring, until the sauce thickens. Spoon the mixture over the hot cooked rice.

Yield: 6 servings. *Each serving provides: 239 cal, 22 g pro, 1.4 g sat fat, 4.4 g unsat fat, 45 mg chol, 312 mg sodium.*

Chicken with Grapes

So easy, so quick, so good! And so few calories!

1 tablespoon chicken fat or
   peanut oil
4 chicken breasts, split,
   boned, and skinned;
   reserve the skin
1 clove garlic, minced
1 cup chicken or vegetable
   broth

1 tablespoon arrowroot or
   cornstarch
½ teaspoon freshly ground
   pepper
½ teaspoon dried thyme
¼ teaspoon ground ginger
1 cup seedless grapes
2 tablespoons finely chopped
   parsley

In a large skillet, render the chicken skin. Remove all but 1 tablespoon of the fat, or use 1 tablespoon of peanut oil.

Brown the chicken breasts on both sides and remove from the skillet. Remove the pan from the heat. Add the garlic. Dissolve the arrowroot or cornstarch in a few tablespoons of broth and add to the skillet. Stir to blend. Add the remaining stock and stir over moderate heat until the mixture boils. Reduce the heat to simmer; add the pepper, ginger, and thyme; and return the chicken to the skillet. Cover and simmer for about 30 minutes or until the chicken is tender. Add the grapes and parsley and continue cooking until the grapes are warm.

Yield: 8 servings. *Each serving provides: 179 cal, 26 g pro, 1.4 g sat fat, 3.7 g unsat fat, 45 mg chol, 280 mg sodium.*

Chicken with Apricots

A delightful one-pot dinner. Apricots bring a festive touch and lots of blood-building iron. The rice cooked in the broth contributes a delectable flavor and lots of cholesterol-lowering rice bran.

1 3-pound broiler-fryer, cut in 8 pieces
1 teaspoon dried oregano
1½ cups sliced onions
1 teaspoon herbal seasoning
¼ teaspoon freshly ground pepper
⅛ teaspoon cayenne
½ teaspoon saffron threads (optional)
1 cup raw brown rice
2 cups reduced-sodium chicken broth
⅔ cup dried apricots
1 tablespoon lemon juice

Wash and wipe dry the chicken pieces.

Heat, and spray a 6-quart Dutch oven with nonstick cooking spray. Brown the chicken a few pieces at a time, until golden-brown all over. Remove the chicken as it browns.

Preheat the oven to 350°F.

Add the oregano and onions to the Dutch oven. Sauté, stirring over medium heat, until golden—about 3 minutes.

Add seasonings and saffron if you are using it, and rice to the Dutch oven. Cook, stirring, until the rice is golden—about 6 minutes.

Add the chicken broth, apricots, and lemon juice to the rice mixture. Add the chicken pieces. Bring to a boil.

Transfer the pot to the oven and bake, covered, about 1 hour, or until the chicken is tender. Serve hot, directly from the Dutch oven, or arrange the rice on a platter, placing the apricots around the rice and the chicken on top.

Yield: 6 servings. *Each serving of chicken with rice and apricots provides: 241 cal, 11.8 g pro, 2.6 g sat fat, 9.5 g unsat fat, 71 mg chol, 200 mg sodium.*

Cold Chicken with Avocado Sauce

Velvety sensual avocado teams up with chicken to form a lovely blend of flavors and texture.

2 *whole chicken breasts, halved, boned, and skinned*
water to cover

4 *cloves garlic*
½ *teaspoon thyme, tarragon, or oregano*

SAUCE

½ *cup mashed avocado*
1 *tablespoon lemon juice*

1 *tablespoon tahini*

TO MAKE THE CHICKEN: Flatten each chicken breast with a mallet or a heavy skillet until about ¼-inch thick. Place in a skillet and pour in just enough water to cover. Add the whole garlic cloves and the herb of your choice. Bring to a boil, then reduce to simmer, covered, for about 10 minutes or until the chicken is tender. Remove the chicken from the broth and chill.

(continued)

TO MAKE THE SAUCE: Combine the avocado, lemon juice, and tahini in a small bowl and beat until smooth. Spread some of the sauce over each breast and roll up. Use a toothpick in each roll to hold its shape. Garnish the top of each with a spoonful of sauce. Serve immediately.

Yield: 4 servings. *Each serving provides: 212 cal, 27 g pro, 2.5 sat fat, 9 g unsat fat, no chol, no sodium.*

Savory Grapefruit Chicken

Grapefruit contributes a palate-pleasing tartness and lots of vitamin C to help you get more mileage out of the minerals in the chicken. It also provides the very important bioflavonoids that help to keep your capillary walls strong.

1 chicken—about 3 pounds—cut in pieces

½ cup plus 2 tablespoons grapefruit juice, divided

2 tablespoons sliced scallions

1 tablespoon chopped parsley

¾ teaspoon herbal seasoning

¼ teaspoon dried marjoram

⅛ teaspoon freshly ground pepper

⅛ teaspoon poultry seasoning

1 large green pepper, cut in chunks

1½ teaspoons arrowroot or cornstarch

1 cup grapefruit sections

Brown the chicken pieces under the broiler, then place them in a large skillet. Add ½ cup of the grapefruit juice, and the scallions, parsley, herbal seasoning, marjoram, pepper, and poultry seasoning.

Cover and simmer for 15 minutes. Add the green pepper. Cover and simmer for 15 minutes longer or until the chicken is tender.

With a slotted spoon, remove the chicken and green pepper to a serving platter. Dissolve the arrowroot or cornstarch in the remaining 2 tablespoons of grapefruit juice; add this to the skillet and stir until the sauce boils and thickens. Add the grapefruit sections. Pour the sauce over the chicken.

Yield: 4 servings. *Each serving provides: 152 cal, 25 g pro, 1.28 g sat fat, 2.07 g unsat fat, 70 mg chol, 70 mg sodium.*

Granny Smith Chicken

A very-low-calorie, delightful combination of orchard and barnyard.

1 3½- to 4-pound chicken, cut in 8 pieces
1 teaspoon herbal seasoner
¼ teaspoon freshly ground pepper
1 cup mushrooms, quartered
2 leeks, washed and chopped
1½ cups chicken broth

¼ cup apple juice or cider
1 large Granny Smith apple, unpeeled, cored, and cut into ¼-inch wedges
1 tablespoon lemon juice
2 tablespoons arrowroot or cornstarch

Wash and dry the chicken pieces. Remove all visible fat.

In a large skillet over medium-high heat, render the fat. Sprinkle the chicken with the seasoner and pepper.

(continued)

Remove all but 1 tablespoon of fat from the skillet. Brown chicken pieces, half at a time, on both sides—about 10 minutes. Remove the chicken pieces to the platter as they brown.

Remove all but 2 tablespoons of drippings from the skillet. Sauté the mushrooms and leeks for 3 minutes. Add 1 cup of chicken broth and the apple juice or cider, stirring to loosen the delicious brown bits from the bottom of the skillet.

Return the chicken to the skillet and bring the liquid just to a boil, then reduce the heat and simmer, covered, for 20 minutes. Add the apple and lemon juice. Cook covered 3 minutes longer or until the apple is tender.

In a small bowl, blend the remaining chicken broth with the arrowroot or cornstarch. Cook another minute or until the sauce thickens.

Yield: 4 servings. *Each serving provides: 213 cal, 26 g pro, 1.28 g sat fat, 2.6 g unsat fat, 74 mg chol, 317 mg sodium.*

Exotic Flavored Pineapple Chicken

We call this the "chicken that went to college." It's so easy to put together for an impromptu meal for hungry teenagers, and it gets its marvelous, exotic flavor from incongruous ingredients that can be found in practically every pantry.

6 chicken legs (thighs and drumsticks) or 2 fryers, disjointed

1 cup ketchup (preferably homemade, see Index)

1 can (20 ounces) crushed pineapple, drained

2 cloves garlic, minced

½ teaspoon ground ginger

¼ teaspoon dry mustard

1 teaspoon herbal seasoning

1 cup freshly brewed decaffeinated coffee

Place the chicken in a baking dish or roasting pan. Set aside. Combine all the remaining ingredients in a bowl. Pour this mixture over the chicken.

At this point you can cover the pan and allow it to marinate overnight in the refrigerator, or you can place the pan in a 350°F oven and bake for about an hour or until tender, basting frequently with the delicious sauce.

Yield: 6 servings. *Each serving provides: 230 cal, 28 g pro, 2 g sat fat, 4 g unsat fat, 75 mg chol, 75 mg sodium.*

10

EXOTIC ETHNIC DISHES

You can take a gastronomic tour of the world without a backpack and without a travel guide. The recipes in this chapter bring you the fiery taste of Mexico, the peanut-flavored delights of Indonesia, the Old World nostalgic spice of Hungary, the luscious black olives and spicy spaghetti of Italy. All the palate-pleasing delights of a culinary adventure without leaving home, but with a healthy difference: Fat content has been slashed, sugar has been eliminated, and cooking procedures have been simplified. Enjoy!

Hungarian Chicken Paprikash

The sauce permeates the chicken and the noodles for a full-bodied dish of Old World flavor. It can also be served on brown rice or millet for a change of texture and more fiber.

2 broiler-fryers, cut up	1 teaspoon herbal seasoning
1 cup chopped onions	¼ teaspoon pepper
2 tablespoons paprika	1 can (8 ounces) tomatoes
1 tablespoon whole wheat flour	1 pound broad noodles, cooked

Remove all visible fat and some of the skin from the chickens.

In a large skillet, render the chicken fat and skin. Brown the chicken pieces in the rendered fat. Remove the browned chicken from the skillet and sauté the onions in the pan drippings until soft. Stir in the paprika and the flour. Cook, stirring constantly, for 1 minute. Stir in the herbal seasoning, pepper, and tomatoes. Break up the tomatoes with a wooden spoon.

Add the chicken and giblets (except the liver). Turn to coat each piece. Cover the skillet and simmer for 20 minutes. Turn the chicken pieces and add the liver. Simmer 15 minutes longer or until the chicken is tender.

Place the hot noodles on a serving platter. Arrange the chicken on the noodles. Bring the sauce in the skillet to a boil. Spoon the hot sauce over the noodles and chicken before serving.

Yield: 8 servings. *Each serving provides: 179 cal, 48 g pro, 1 g sat fat, 2 g unsat fat, 75 mg chol, 150 mg sodium.*

Latin Chicken with Spaghetti

A colorful and flavorful bless-your-heart dish enriched with oat bran and lecithin and embellished with red pimentos and black olives.

2 broiler-fryers (about 2½ to 3
    pounds each), cut in
    serving-size pieces
½ cup whole wheat flour
½ cup oat bran
2 tablespoons lecithin
    granules
1 teaspoon herbal seasoning
¼ teaspoon freshly ground
    pepper
2 cloves garlic, minced

⅓ cup chopped parsley
½ teaspoon poultry seasoning
    dash Tabasco sauce
1 cup dry white wine
¼ cup pitted black olives, sliced
½ cup sliced mushrooms
1 jar (4 ounces) red pimentos,
    drained and cut into
    1-inch pieces
1 pound thin spaghetti,
    cooked

Remove all visible fat and some of the skin from the chickens. Render the fat and skin in a large, heavy skillet. Remove the chicken cracklings and reserve for another use.

On waxed paper, blend together the flour, oat bran, lecithin granules, herbal seasoning, and pepper. Roll the chicken in the seasoned flour mixture, then brown it in the rendered fat.

Blend together the garlic, parsley, poultry seasoning, Tabasco sauce, and wine. Pour over the browned chicken and simmer for 5 minutes.

Scatter the olives, mushrooms, and pimento over the chicken. Cover the skillet and cook over moderately low heat for 30 minutes or until the chicken is tender.

Place the hot spaghetti on a serving dish. Top with the chicken pieces. Pour the hot wine sauce over all.

Yield: 8 servings. *Each serving provides: 270 cal, 48 g pro, 4 g sat fat, 8 g unsat fat, 75 mg chol, 245 mg sodium.*

Chicken Cacciatore

1 broiler-fryer, cut up
½ cup chopped onions
½ teaspoon herbal seasoning
¼ teaspoon freshly ground
    pepper
1 clove garlic, minced

1 can (1-pound) tomatoes
1 tablespoon vinegar
    (preferably balsamic)
½ teaspoon rosemary,
    crumbled
½ teaspoon honey

Remove all visible fat and the fatty pieces of the skin from the chicken and render them in a heavy skillet.

Remove the browned cracklings and all but 1 tablespoon of fat from the skillet. Brown the onions in the fat and remove.

Sprinkle the chicken with the herbal seasoning and the pepper. Add another tablespoon of chicken fat or oil and brown the chicken pieces in the skillet with the garlic.

Add all the remaining ingredients and the browned onions to the skillet. Cover and simmer for 30 minutes or until the chicken is tender.

Yield: 4 servings. *Each serving provides: 170 cal, 22 g pro, 1.5 g sat fat, 2.5 g unsat fat, 65 mg chol, 140 mg sodium.*

Sombrero Baked Chicken
Flavored with Cinnamon and Carob

For those who like it hot, this dish will hit the spot. Serve with a cool cucumber salad and a Mexican brown rice and cream-style corn casserole.

1 broiler-fryer (about 2½ to 3 pounds), cut in serving-size pieces
1 teaspoon herbal seasoning
¼ teaspoon freshly ground pepper
1 red or green pepper, cut in strips
1 can (8 ounces) tomato sauce

2 tablespoons apricot conserves or orange marmalade
1 tablespoon carob powder or unsweetened cocoa
½ teaspoon Tabasco® sauce
½ teaspoon cinnamon
2 teaspoons sesame seed

Remove all visible fat and some of the fatty skin from the chicken pieces; reserve for future use. Place the chicken pieces in a baking dish in a single layer and sprinkle with the herbal seasoning and pepper.

Place the pepper strips over the chicken.

In a bowl, combine the tomato sauce, apricot conserves or orange marmalade, carob or cocoa, Tabasco® sauce, and cinnamon. Sprinkle with the sesame seeds. Cover with foil or parchment paper and bake at 375°F for 45 minutes. Remove the foil or parchment paper and bake 15 minutes longer.

Yield: 8 servings. *Each serving provides: 178 cal, 22 g pro, 1.5 g sat fat, 2.9 g unsat fat, 70 mg chol, 305 mg sodium.*

Iranian Chicken with Pistachios and Sweet Rice

2 broiler-fryers (about 2½ to 3 pounds each), cut in serving-size pieces

3 carrots, scraped clean and thinly sliced

4 cups chicken broth, divided

½ cup chopped almonds, lightly toasted (2 minutes in the microwave or 7 minutes in a 350°F oven)

1 tablespoon grated orange rind

2 tablespoons apricot conserves or orange marmalade

2 medium onions, thinly sliced

½ cup chicken broth or water

2 cups long-grain brown rice

⅛ teaspoon freshly ground pepper

½ teaspoon paprika

1 teaspoon herbal seasoning

4 tablespoons unsalted pistachio nuts, chopped

Remove all visible fat and some of the fatty skin from each chicken. In a heavy saucepan, render the fat of one chicken. Remove the crispy cracklings when golden, and reserve.

Add the sliced carrots. Cook over low heat until crisp-tender. Add 1 cup of chicken stock and the almonds, orange rind, and conserves or marmalade. Set aside.

In a heavy 2-quart saucepan with a tight-fitting lid, cook the sliced onions in ½ cup of chicken broth or water until the onions are soft but not browned. Add 3 cups of stock and bring to a boil. Add the rice, herbal seasoning, and carrot mixture. Mix to blend the ingredients, cover tightly, and cook over low heat until the liquid is absorbed and rice is tender, about 40 minutes.

While the rice is cooking, render the fat of the other chicken in a large skillet with a lid. Brown both chickens all over. Sprinkle with the pepper, paprika, and herbal seasoning, and cook over low heat for 10 minutes. Turn the chicken pieces, cover again, and cook 10 minutes longer or until the chicken is tender and the juices run clear.

Spoon 1 cup of the rice mixture on each plate. Top with a serving of chicken, and garnish with chicken cracklings or toasted pistachio nuts.

Yield: 8 servings. *Each serving of chicken and rice provides: 400 cal, 29 g pro, 2 g sat fat, 8 g unsat fat, 70 mg chol, 196 mg sodium.*

Indonesian Peanut-Studded Chicken

The crunchy oat bran and chopped peanut overcoat on each piece of this moist, flavorful chicken make this a special-occasion dish. Your bypass friends will love it. Serve with a tossed salad and a sweet potato and apple casserole.

1 broiler-fryer, cut up
1 teaspoon herbal seasoner
¼ teaspoon freshly ground
    pepper
¾ cup oat bran
1 egg white

¾ cup apricot conserves or
    orange marmalade
1 teaspoon dry mustard
2 cloves garlic, minced
½ cup peanuts, finely chopped

Dust the chicken with the herbal seasoner and the pepper. Place the oat bran on a sheet of waxed paper.

In a soup bowl or on a pie plate, combine the egg white, conserves or marmalade, mustard, and garlic.

Put the chopped peanuts on another piece of waxed paper.

Dip the chicken pieces first in the oat bran, then in the egg mixture, then roll in the chopped peanuts. Place the chicken in a single layer in a baking dish. Bake at 375°F for 40 minutes or until the chicken is tender and the peanuts are golden.

Yield: 4 servings. *Each serving provides: 438 cal, 32 g pro, 2 g sat fat, 12 g unsat fat, 70 mg chol, 117 mg sodium.*

Poached Chicken Parisienne

Cool and fruity—a wonderful dish for a patio lunch when the thermometer soars. Apricots are rich in cancer-inhibiting vitamin A and in magnesium, a mineral necessary for the proper functioning of the nerves and muscles, including the heart. Grapes are an excellent source of potassium, especially needed during the hot months when it is depleted through perspiration.

3 *whole chicken breasts (about 12 ounces each)*	1 *cup chopped celery*
5 *or 6 celery leaves*	1 *cup seedless green grapes, halved*
2 *teaspoons no-salt herbal seasoner*	*cucumber dressing (recipe follows)*
6 *peppercorns*	*romaine or Bibb lettuce*
2 *bay leaves*	6 *apricots, washed, halved, and pitted*
1 *cup chicken broth*	

In a large skillet or saucepan, combine the chicken breasts, celery leaves, herbal seasoner, peppercorns, bay leaves, and chicken broth. Bring to a boil. Cover and simmer for 30 minutes or until the meat is tender.

Allow the chicken to cook in the broth until it is easy to handle, then remove and pull off the skin. Remove the meat from the bones and cut it in cubes. Reserve the broth for another use.

In a large bowl, combine the cut-up chicken, celery, and grapes. Drizzle with about half of the cucumber dressing (see the following recipe). Toss lightly to mix, and chill at least an hour to blend the flavors.

To serve, line a large bowl with lettuce, pile the chicken mixture in the center, frame with the apricot halves, and serve with the remaining dressing.

Yield: 6 servings. *Each serving with 2 tablespoons of dressing provides: 143 cal, 18.6 g pro, 0.88 g sat fat, 1.66 g unsat fat, 66 mg chol, 169.3 mg sodium.*

Cucumber Dressing

⅓ cup reduced-fat mayonnaise
   or salad dressing
1 teaspoon no-salt herbal
   seasoning
1 teaspoon chopped fresh dill
   or ⅓ teaspoon dried

¼ teaspoon pepper
⅓ cup lemon juice
1 cup puréed cucumber
1 small cucumber, pared and
   diced

Combine all the ingredients and chill at least 1 hour.

Yield: 2 cups. *Each tablespoon provides: about 10 cal, 0.5 g fat, no chol, 17 mg sodium.*

South of the Border Curried Chicken with Rice and Jamaican Rum

Play rumba music while you enjoy this whole meal in a dish. Both onions and garlic tend to lower cholesterol levels; tomatoes provide lots of vitamin A, potassium, and iron; brown rice is a powerhouse of morale-boosting B vitamins and provides valuable rice bran, credited with lowering harmful cholesterol levels.

2 broiler-fryers (2½ to 3 pounds each), cut in serving-size pieces
1 cup finely chopped onions
2 cloves garlic, minced
¼ cup chopped green peppers
1½ cups canned tomatoes
½ teaspoon freshly ground pepper

2 teaspoons curry powder
½ teaspoon oregano
1 teaspoon no-salt herbal seasoning
5 cups low-sodium chicken broth, divided
3 tablespoons Jamaican rum
2 tablespoons paprika
1½ cups brown rice

Remove from the chickens all the visible fat and some of the fatty skin and render them in a heavy skillet. Remove the chicken cracklings and all but 2 tablespoons of chicken fat.

Sauté the onions, garlic, and green peppers in the skillet for about 10 minutes. Add the tomatoes, ground pepper, herbal seasoning, curry powder, oregano, and 2 cups of the broth. Cook over low heat for about 20 minutes. Add the rum and cook 10 minutes longer.

While the sauce is cooking, prepare the chickens and rice. Sprinkle the chicken with the paprika and broil until tender.

Bring the remaining broth to a boil. Stir in the rice. Cover and cook over low heat for 40 minutes or until tender. Watch carefully and add a little more water or broth if necessary.

Place the rice in a heavy saucepan or Dutch oven. Arrange the chicken over the rice. Pour the sauce over all. Cover and cook over low heat for 10 minutes.

Yield: 8 servings. *Each serving provides: 261 cal, 24 g pro, 1.5 g sat fat, 3.2 g unsat fat, 70 mg chol, 251 mg sodium.*

Yorkshire Batter-Baked Chicken

The batter, made with oat bran, whole wheat flour, and wheat germ, contributes a pleasant crunch, lots of heart-healthy fiber, and the whole family of B vitamins.

1 broiler-fryer (about 2½ to 3 pounds), cut in serving pieces

2 tablespoons oat bran (for coating)

2 tablespoons wheat germ or whole wheat flour (for coating)

1 teaspoon salt-free herbal seasoning (for coating)

½ teaspoon freshly ground pepper (for coating)

4 eggs

1½ cups low-sodium chicken broth

1½ cups whole wheat pastry flour (for batter)

1 teaspoon paprika

1 teaspoon sodium-free herbal seasoning (for batter)

¼ teaspoon pepper (for batter)

(continued)

Cut from the chicken all the visible fat and some of the fatty skin and render them in a heavy skillet. Remove and reserve the chicken cracklings.

On waxed paper, combine the oat bran, wheat germ or whole wheat flour, and herbal seasoning for the coating. Coat the chicken and brown the pieces well in the fat in the skillet. Remove the chicken from the skillet but do not discard the pan drippings.

TO MAKE THE BATTER: In a medium-size bowl, beat the eggs until light. Stir in the chicken broth. Combine the flour, paprika, herbal seasoning, and pepper, and add to the egg mixture. Beat just until the batter is smooth. Stir in the pan drippings and the reserved cracklings.

Preheat the oven to 375°F. Coat a 13 x 9 x 2-inch baking dish with no-fat cooking spray and heat the dish in the oven.

Pour the batter into the heated baking dish and arrange the chicken pieces in the batter.

Bake for 45 minutes or until golden and puffy.

Yield: 6 servings. *Each serving provides: 270 cal, 24 g pro, 1.2 g sat fat, 2.2 g unsat fat, 162 mg chol, 133 mg sodium.*

Left Bank Dijon Chicken

This is not mild-flavored, but it isn't tongue-stinging hot, either. You can safely serve it to family or friends of varying taste buds. They'll love it!

2 broiler-fryers (about 2½ to 3 pounds each), cut into serving-size pieces
¾ cup low-sodium chicken broth
¾ cup tarragon vinegar

3 tablespoons salt-free Dijon mustard
1 teaspoon salt-free herbal seasoning
½ teaspoon freshly ground pepper

Remove all visible fat and some of the fatty skin from the chicken and reserve for another use.

In a large bowl, combine the broth, vinegar, mustard, herbal seasoning, and pepper. Add the chicken and marinate at least 2 hours in the refrigerator, turning once.

Place the chicken pieces skin side down on the broiler rack. Broil 6 inches from the heat for 15 minutes. Turn and broil 20 to 30 minutes longer, basting frequently until the chicken is tender.

Yield: 8 servings. *Each serving provides: 131 cal, 21.5 g pro, 1.5 g sat fat, 2.5 g unsat fat, 70 mg chol, 109 mg sodium.*

Chicken Tel Aviv

So simple to prepare and so good! Serve with thin spaghetti or couscous to mop up the delicious sauce.

1 broiler-fryer (2½ to 3 pounds), cut in serving-size pieces

1 cup tomato sauce with mushrooms (Rokeach, no salt added)

1 leek, thinly sliced (1 cup) or 1 cup chopped onions

1 can (3 or 4 ounces) chopped mushrooms

¼ cup chicken broth or water

2 tablespoons lemon juice

Remove all the visible fat from the chicken; reserve for another use. Arrange the chicken in a 13 x 9 x 2-inch baking dish.

In a medium-size bowl, combine the tomato sauce with mushrooms, leek or onions, chopped mushrooms, chicken broth or water, and lemon juice. Spoon over the chicken pieces.

Bake at 375°F for 1 hour or until the chicken is tender and nicely browned.

Yield: 4 servings. *Each serving provides: 180 cal, 21.6 g pro, 1.5 g sat fat, 2.5 g unsat fat, 70 mg chol, 198 mg sodium.*

Chicken Sabra
with Bing Cherries and Brown Rice

Delightful to behold and delicious to eat. Definitely a celebration dish.

1 broiler-fryer (3½ to 4
   pounds), cut in
   serving-size pieces
1 teaspoon no-salt herbal
   seasoning
1 teaspoon paprika
2 large onions, sliced
½ cup chicken stock

2 cups pitted bing cherries,
   fresh or frozen
1 tablespoon honey
2 tablespoons orange, apple,
   or apricot juice
1½ cups long-grain brown rice
4 cups water

Remove all the visible fat and some of the fatty skin and render it in a large, heavy skillet. Remove the chicken cracklings and all but 2 tablespoons of the chicken fat; reserve for another use.

Add the chicken pieces to the hot fat. Cook for about 5 minutes on each side to brown. Remove the chicken, and brown the onions in the skillet. Return the chicken to the skillet and add the chicken stock and herbal seasoning. Bring to a boil, then reduce the heat to low. Cover the skillet and simmer for 30 minutes or until the chicken is fork-tender.

While the chicken is simmering, combine the cherries, honey, and 2 tablespoons of fruit juice in a saucepan over very low heat.

Partially cook the rice by combining it with 4 cups of water in a large saucepan. Bring to a boil, then reduce the heat and simmer for 20 minutes. Drain the rice through a strainer, reserving the liquid.

(continued)

Combine the pan drippings and 1 cup of the reserved rice water in a large, ovenproof casserole. Spreading it out evenly, put half the rice in the casserole. Add the chicken pieces, onions, and half the cherries. Arrange the rest of the rice on top of the mixture. Add the remaining cherries with their cooking liquid. Cover the casserole and simmer for 20 minutes or until the rice is tender.

Arrange half the rice on your prettiest serving platter. Arrange the chicken pieces and the onions on top of the bed of rice. Top the chicken with the cherries and half the remaining rice. Make an attractive border with the rest of the rice.

Yield: 6 servings. *Each serving provides: 327 cal, 22.6 g pro, 1 g sat fat, 2 g unsat fat, 70 mg chol, 66 mg sodium.*

Canton Chicken with Almonds

Serve with bowls of hot brown rice and toasty oat bran crunch for a delicious meal that is high in fiber and nutrient-rich.

2 tablespoons chicken fat or olive oil (or 1 tablespoon of each)
1 teaspoon no-salt herbal seasoning
2 cups diced raw chicken
1 tablespoon reduced-sodium soy sauce
1 cup diced celery
½ cup canned mushrooms
1 cup cooked peas
1 cup hot chicken stock or boiling water
1 tablespoon arrowroot or cornstarch
¼ cup cold water
½ cup toasted whole almonds

Heat the chicken fat or olive oil in a large skillet or a wok. Add the seasoning and the chicken and sauté for about 3 minutes. Add the soy sauce and stir well. Add the celery, mushrooms, peas, and stock or water very slowly and stir well. Cover and cook for 4 minutes.

Mix the arrowroot or cornstarch with the cold water and add to the chicken mixture. Lower the heat and simmer until the gravy thickens. Remove from the heat and transfer to a serving plate. Sprinkle with toasted whole almonds.

Yield: 4 servings. *Each serving provides: 310 cal, 35.4 g pro, 3.38 g sat fat, 15 g unsat fat, 66 mg chol, 325 mg sodium.*

Israeli Chicken Bake
with Matzoh and Dill

Delicious anytime, but especially welcome as a change from roast chicken for Passover.

2 cups cooked diced chicken
1 onion, finely chopped
6 eggs, beaten
3 tablespoons chopped parsley
3 teaspoons dried dill
1½ teaspoons no-salt herbal
    seasoning

½ teaspoon black pepper
3 squares matzoh, preferably
    whole wheat
2 cups chicken stock
3 teaspoons oil or chicken fat

(continued)

In a large mixing bowl, combine the chicken, onion, eggs, parsley, dill, herbal seasoning, and pepper.

Pour 2 cups of chicken stock in a flat soup plate. Moisten the matzohs well in the chicken stock.

Preheat the oven to 400°F. Place one teaspoon of oil or chicken fat in a 9-inch-square baking dish and heat the fat in the preheating oven.

Lay one matzoh on the bottom of the baking dish and spread half of the chicken mixture over it. Cover with a second moistened matzoh, spread the remaining chicken mixture over this, and top with the third matzoh. Dribble another teaspoon of fat over the top and bake for 15 minutes. Add the remaining fat and bake until the top is browned—approximately 15 minutes.

Yield: 6 servings. *Each serving provides: 339 cal, 35 g pro, 4.2 g sat fat, 8.9 g unsat fat, 266 mg chol, 298 mg sodium.*

Coke 'n' Chicken

What a combination! The following recipe is adapted from one that won top honors in a chicken recipe contest held in Israel. It sounded bizarre, so I wanted to try it. But I had no Coca-Cola, so I substituted unsweetened pineapple juice. For the ketchup, I substituted tomato sauce. I was amazed at how good it was. Then I tried the original Coca-Cola version. It was very tasty. For a once-in-a-while lark, here's the Coca-Cola version. For better nutritional value, try my revised version.

2 medium-size onions,
  chopped
½ cup Coca-Cola Classic or ½
  cup unsweetened
  pineapple juice
¼ cup ketchup or ¼ cup
  tomato sauce
2 tablespoons vinegar,
  preferably balsamic
½ cup fruit juice–sweetened
  apricot conserves

2 tablespoons Worcestershire
  sauce
½ teaspoon chili powder
3 medium-size sweet
  potatoes, cut in ½-inch
  chunks
2 small chickens (about 2½
  pounds each), cut in
  serving pieces

In a heavy saucepan, combine all ingredients except the chickens and the sweet potatoes. Bring to a boil, reduce the heat, and simmer, covered, for about 30 minutes, or until the sauce is thickened, while stirring occasionally.

Arrange the chicken pieces in an ovenproof casserole. Arrange the sweet potato chunks around the border of the dish. Pour the Worcestershire sauce over the chicken and over the sweet potatoes. Bake in a 350°F oven for 1 hour or until the chicken is tender.

Yield: 8 servings. *Each serving provides: 235 cal, 39 g pro, 2 g sat fat, 3.5 g unsat fat, 70 mg chol, 164 mg sodium.*

Toasty Persian Chicken Balls

This is a great appetizer, small enough for the calorie-counter and hearty enough for the hungry bears. I like to keep a supply at the ready in the freezer. Unexpected company always marvels at how I whip them up so fast.

1 cup cooked chicken, boned	1 tablespoon curry powder
2 teaspoons chopped parsley	prepared mustard
2 teaspoons oat bran	1 egg, slightly beaten
2 teaspoons minced onion	2 teaspoons sesame seeds

In a chopping bowl or food processor, chop the chicken fine. Add the parsley, oat bran, onion, and curry powder, and process to blend the ingredients.

Add only enough mustard to make a moist paste. Shape into small balls, the size of a hickory nut, roll in the egg and then in the sesame seeds. Freeze or refrigerate for 1 hour or longer. Toast in a 450°F oven for 10 to 15 minutes.

Yield: Approximately 36 toasties. *Each toasty provides: 10 cal, 1 g pro, hardly a trace of fat, 2 mg chol, 8 mg sodium.*

Moroccan Chicken Stew
with Olives and Avocado

Avocados and olives bring a powerhouse of fountain-of-youth nutrients to this fantastic dish. Don't limit this dish to special occasions; it makes every occasion special.

2 chickens (about 3 pounds each), cut in serving pieces, skin removed and reserved
1 large onion, chopped
2 cloves garlic, minced
½ cup orange juice
1 teaspoon herbal seasoning
⅛ teaspoon freshly ground pepper

1 tablespoon fresh tarragon or ½ teaspoon dried
1 lemon, washed and thinly sliced
¼ cup fresh parsley, chopped
1 cup pitted black olives
1 avocado, peeled, cubed, and tossed in orange juice

Remove all visible fat from the chicken. Cut the chicken skin in smallish pieces. In a large, heavy skillet, render the fat and skin until the cracklings are brown and crisp. If you get more than 2 tablespoons of fat, remove it along with the cracklings and reserve for another use. If you get less than 2 tablespoons, add a little olive oil or canola oil to make up the difference.

Add the cut-up chicken to the skillet and brown on all sides. Add the onion, garlic, orange juice, herbal seasoning, pepper, and lemon. Cook for 15 minutes. Stir in the parsley and olives. Cover and cook over moderate heat for about 25 minutes or until the chicken is cooked.

(continued)

109

Stir occasionally and add water or chicken broth if it seems dry. Remove the chicken to a serving dish and spoon the olive mixture over it. Top with the cubed avocado.

Yield: 8 servings. *Each serving provides: 215 cal, 31.5 g pro, 3.5 g sat fat, 4.5 g unsat fat, 70 mg chol, 135 mg sodium.*

Farfel Chicken Casserole

This is a great dish for Passover but can be enjoyed anytime you want to make a little leftover chicken go a long, long way. It can be made with macaroni for non-Passover use.

*1 to 2 teaspoons chicken fat
    or peanut oil
1 large onion, diced
1 cup chicken soup or stock
1 cup vegetable juice, stock,
    or water
2 cups cut-up cooked chicken
2 cups cooked sliced carrots
    or other cooked
    vegetables*

*1 cup diced celery
1½ cups matzoh farfel
    (available at Jewish
    delicatessens), or break
    whole wheat matzohs
    into pieces no larger than
    a thumbnail
pepper and paprika*

In a large, heavy saucepan, heat the chicken fat or peanut oil. Add the onion and sauté until transparent but not brown. Add the chicken soup or stock and the vegetable juice, stock, or water. Cook for about 5 minutes to make a sauce.

In a 2-quart casserole, arrange the chicken, vegetables, matzoh farfel, and the sauce in alternate layers. Season to taste with pepper and paprika. Cover and bake in a preheated 350°F oven for about 30 minutes.

Yield: 6 servings. *Each serving provides: 154 cal, 16 g pro, 1.2 g sat fat, 3 g unsat fat, 66 mg chol, 204 mg sodium.*

11

Turkey

You can't mention Thanksgiving without evoking the tantalizing aroma of a succulent turkey. And when you think of turkey, you recall the holiday nostalgia of family reunions around the Thanksgiving table.

Thanksgiving comes but once a year. But there's no reason at all why we can't enjoy turkey much more frequently and be thankful each time it shows up on the menu. The big gobbler just happens to be a very good nutritional buy—and the answer to the prayers of the epicurean waistline-watcher. It is extremely low in fat and very high in protein.

Turkey comes in sizes that might be too large for your own family. But when you consider that turkey freezes well and can then be incorporated into a great variety of fantastic dishes, your investment in the big bird is more than justified.

Turkey is high in essential fatty acids, yet one of the lowest of all meats in calories. It is also an excellent source of riboflavin (B_2), which is especially important to your skin and eyes, and niacin, which is necessary to a host of mental functions and to the reduction of high cholesterol levels.

So turkey on the menu does help to keep those faces glowing, eyes sparkling, and the conversation bright and merry. (All the time you thought it was your great cooking!) Not that cooking it right doesn't help. It sure does. So here are some hints:

If you can get a fresh turkey from someone you know who raises them naturally, you're in luck. But fresh turkeys are hard to come by, so you will probably settle for a frozen one.

Before you cook it, thaw it in the refrigerator. A large bird takes two to four days, half that time for a small bird. If, when you are ready to cook it, the turkey is not completely thawed, then put it under cold running water to finish the job.

Never let the thawed bird stand around at room temperature. It should go from freezer to refrigerator to sink to oven. Prepare the stuffing ahead of time but never stuff the bird until it's ready for the oven.

COOKING THE BIG BIRD
Start the turkey early enough in the day so you can roast it in a slow oven—325°F. Slow oven roasting preserves more moisture and juices and does the least violence to the many nutrients in the turkey meat. (Figure on 20 minutes for every pound.) Plan your roasting time so that the turkey will be done about a half hour before its grand entrance. The rest period before curtain time makes carving easy and gives you time to prepare the gravy.

If you plan to stuff the bird, fill it loosely with the stuffing of your choice. Remember, it will expand. Don't forget to stuff the neck cavity, too. An average-size turkey (up to 12 pounds) will take 2 to 3 quarts of stuffing. It's a good idea to make extra stuffing and bake it separately in a casserole or as individual servings in muffin tins, to be used at a later meal when the turkey comes back for an encore.

After stuffing the bird, close the openings with skewers or sew with strong white thread, and buss securely.

Preheat the oven to 325°F.

To put a becoming blush on your turkey, try this method, which always gets a standing ovation at our house.

In a small bowl, combine these ingredients: several cloves of crushed garlic; the juice of 2 lemons; 4 tablespoons of tomato paste; and 1 teaspoon each of poultry seasoning or sage, thyme, marjoram, herbal seasoning, and paprika. These amounts are for a 10-pound turkey, so judge accordingly.

Rub the turkey inside and outside with this mixture, then place it, breast side up, on a rack in a roaster. Roast, uncovered, basting about every half hour with the pan drippings. If the turkey browns too quickly while roasting, tent it with parchment paper or aluminum foil.

The best way to determine doneness is to insert a thermometer in the thigh muscle. It should register 185°F. Another test for doneness is to pierce the thigh with the tip of a small, sharp knife. The juices should be clear. If the juices are tinged with pink, roast for about 10 minutes more. When it tests done, transfer to a heated platter and let it rest before carving.

Meanwhile, make the gravy. Pour off all but 2 tablespoons of fat from the roasting pan. Stir about 2 tablespoons of arrowroot, cornstarch, or whole wheat flour into the pan. When it is absorbed, add a cup of hot water or stock. Heat to a boil, stirring constantly with a wire whisk, and incorporate into the liquid all the flavorful, brown crusty pieces on the bottom and sides of the pan. Season to taste, and pour into a heated gravy boat.

ROASTING WITHOUT BASTING

This is a carefree method of achieving luscious juiciness. Prepare the turkey the same as for oven roasting. Moisten a large sheet of parchment paper (available at some department stores and cookware or specialty shops). For large birds, use two widths. Place the turkey breast side up in the middle of the parchment. Bring the long ends up over the breast and overlap 3 inches. Close open ends by folding up the parchment paper to prevent drippings from running into the pan. Now wrap the whole thing in foil in the same manner to keep the parchment intact. The foil does not come in contact with the bird.

Place the wrapped turkey, breast side up, in a roasting pan. No rack is needed. An hour before you expect the bird to be done, fold back the parchment and foil completely to bring a becoming blush and some crispness to the skin. Give it the thermometer or thigh test for doneness. When the juices run clear, your bird is ready for some of the most appreciative exclamations of gustatorial delight that will ever pleasure your soul.

ONCE IS NOT ENOUGH

The turkey was scrumptious, the family loved it. But you still have half a bird left. How shall you fix it? Let me count the ways. There's hash, stew, chop suey, casseroles, stir-fry dishes with vegetables, scrapple, pancakes, crepes, sandwiches, and salads, and whatever else your own creative juices come up with.

(These recipes for leftover turkey can be used for any cooked poultry, whether chicken, capon, goose, duck, or guinea hen.)

SALADS

You can enjoy a turkey salad the day after Thanksgiving or a month after the holiday. Simply pack one cup of cut-up turkey in a carton and freeze. You will always have workable amounts to use in salads, casseroles, to fill crepes, or whatever.

Turkey and Almond Salad

Easy to prepare, light, and yet festive. It's a nice change from the rather heavy Thanksgiving dinner and is most welcome when served the day after the holiday.

2 cups diced cooked turkey
½ cup chopped celery
½ cup slivered or chopped
   almonds, lightly roasted

1 cup presoaked raisins;
   reserve the liquid
⅓ cup reduced-fat mayonnaise
   lettuce

In a glass bowl, combine the turkey, celery, presoaked raisins, and almonds.

In a small dish, mix together ⅓ cup raisin liquid and ⅓ cup mayonnaise. Stir into the turkey mixture. Serve on a bed of dark green lettuce.

Yield: 6 servings. *Each serving provides: 276 cal, 17 g pro, 2.1 g sat fat, 9.2 g unsat fat, 66 mg chol, 182 mg sodium.*

Chinese Turkey Salad

The same turkey has an entirely different flavor when you go Oriental and serve Chinese turkey salad.

1 cup cooked turkey	¼ cup coarsely chopped walnuts
1½ teaspoons Tamari soy sauce	1 cup bean sprouts
½ cup slivered bamboo shoots (optional)	2 tablespoons olive oil
1 cup coarsely shredded lettuce or Chinese cabbage	1½ tablespoons vinegar, preferably rice or balsamic
3 red radishes, thinly sliced	¼ teaspoon powdered ginger lettuce

Cut the turkey into matchstick strips and marinate in the soy sauce for 20 minutes.

In a glass bowl, combine the turkey, bamboo shoots if you're using them, lettuce or cabbage, radishes, walnuts, and sprouts. Toss lightly.

In a small dish, mix together the oil, vinegar, and ginger until well blended. Pour over the salad, tossing lightly to coat the mixture. Serve on a bed of dark green lettuce.

Yield: 4 servings. *Each serving provides: 151 cal, 17 g pro, 3 g fat, 10.3 g unsat fat, 78 mg chol, 41 mg sodium.*

Sparkling Turkey Salad

This is a lovely make-ahead main dish for a special occasion, buffet-bring-a-dish party, luncheon, or festive family dinner.

2½ cups diced cold turkey
1 cup white seedless grapes
½ cup slivered or chopped almonds, lightly toasted
2 tablespoons minced parsley
1 stalk celery, finely chopped
1½ tablespoons gelatin
4 tablespoons cold water

½ cup chicken or turkey stock
¾ cup reduced-calorie mayonnaise or salad dressing
¼ cup no-salt-added Dijon mustard
salad greens

Combine the turkey, grapes, almonds, parsley, and celery.

In a small bowl, soak the gelatin in cold water for 5 minutes, then dissolve in boiling stock.

Combine the mayonnaise and mustard. Add the gelatin stock to the mayonnaise mixture and stir until the mixture begins to thicken. Fold in the turkey mixture. Pack in 1 large mold or in 8 individual molds. Unmold on a bed of salad greens.

Yield: 8 servings. *Each serving provides: 239 cal, 18 g pro, 1.3 g sat fat, 8.1 g unsat fat, 135 mg chol, 239 mg sodium.*

Variation: Line each mold with slices of hard-cooked egg for a lovely effect.

Celebration Turkey Puff Pie

A great dish for big events, a delight to the eye and the palate. Picture a classic cream puff dough flavored with mustard and sesame seeds, filled with turkey and sautéed mushrooms, and topped with crunchy marbles of puffery.

¾ cup water
6 tablespoons tahini (sesame butter)
¾ cup whole wheat flour

3 eggs
1 teaspoon herbal seasoning
½ teaspoon dry mustard
turkey filling (recipe follows)

In a heavy saucepan, bring the water and tahini to a boil. Add the flour all at once. Cook, beating hard with a wooden spoon, until the ingredients are well blended and the mixture leaves the sides of the pan (about 30 seconds).

Remove the pan from the heat and add the eggs, one at a time, beating well after each addition. Mix in the herbal seasoning and mustard.

Coat a 9-inch pie pan with nonstick baking spray. Using ⅔ of the dough, line the bottom and sides of pan. (The dough will be sticky; moisten your fingers or use the back of a spoon to spread.)

Spoon the filling into the crust. Using the remaining dough, form teaspoon-size puffs around the top of the filling. Bake at 375°F for 40 to 45 minutes, until puffed and well browned. Serve piping hot.

Turkey Filling

1 onion, diced
1 cup sliced mushrooms
1 tablespoon chicken fat or
   olive oil

1 tablespoon whole wheat
   flour
½ cup chicken or turkey stock
2 cups cooked turkey, diced

In a large, heavy skillet, sauté the onion and mushrooms in the fat or olive oil. Add the flour and blend. Cook about 1 minute. Add the stock and cook until thickened, about 4 minutes. Stir in the turkey and season to taste. Heat through, then place it in the piecrust.

Yield: 6 servings. *Each serving provides: 235 cal, 22 g pro, 2.6 g sat fat, 7.1 g unsat fat, 135 mg chol, 232 mg sodium.*

Turkey Hash

Once the standby on washday because it is so easy to prepare, but you can serve it with pride any day of the week. Topped with a poached egg, it makes a great breakfast or brunch dish.

1 medium onion, minced
½ green or red pepper, diced
2 tablespoons chicken or
   turkey fat, or olive oil
2 cups cooked diced turkey
   meat
2 cups cooked potatoes, diced,
   or brown rice

¼ cup apple sauce
1 tablespoon minced parsley
1 teaspoon herbal seasoning
⅛ teaspoon freshly ground
   pepper
½ teaspoon poultry seasoning
   or sage
4 poached eggs (optional)

In a large, heavy skillet, stir-fry the onion and pepper in the turkey fat or olive oil, until the onion is golden. Add the remaining ingredients except the eggs. Press down with a spatula and cook, uncovered, without stirring, about 10 minutes, or until a brown crust forms on the bottom. Turn and brown the flip side for about 10 minutes.

Top each serving with a poached egg if you choose.

Yield: 4 servings. *Each serving provides: 272 cal, 28 g pro, 2.7 g sat fat, 8.6 g unsat fat, 70 mg chol, 98 mg sodium.*

Each serving topped with a poached egg provides: 350 cal, 34 g pro, 4.6 g sat fat, 11.5 g unsat fat, 320 mg chol, 157 mg sodium.

Turkey Chow Mein

This hearty, nutritious meal, cooked quickly in a wok, can be served on brown rice, Chinese crispy noodles, or soft cellophane noodles.

1 cup sliced mushrooms
2 onions, minced
3 stalks celery, diced
2 tablespoons chicken or turkey fat or olive oil
2 cups chicken or turkey broth
2 tablespoons Tamari soy sauce
2 tablespoons arrowroot or cornstarch
¼ cup cold water
½ teaspoon herbal seasoning
3 cups cooked turkey, cut in bite-size pieces
1½ cups mung bean sprouts
1 cup water chestnuts, drained, or Jerusalem artichokes, sliced thin
½ cup almonds or cashews, lightly roasted

(continued)

In a heavy skillet or wok, stir-fry the onions, celery, and mushrooms in the fat or olive oil for about 8 minutes or until golden brown. Add the broth and soy sauce. Turn the heat to low, cover, and simmer for about 8 minutes.

Dissolve the arrowroot or cornstarch in cold water, then add to the pot. Continue to cook, stirring, until the liquid is thickened. Lower the heat and add the turkey, bean sprouts, and water chestnuts or Jerusalem artichokes. Continue to heat and stir for about 5 minutes.

Stir in the almonds or cashews and serve over hot brown rice or noodles.

Yield: 6 servings. *Each serving provides: 301.5 cal, 7 g pro, 2.3 g sat fat, 12 g unsat fat, 70 mg chol, 240 mg sodium.*

Polynesian Turkey

A sweet and sour dish that is easy to prepare and always makes a hit. Serve over brown rice or as a topping for baked potatoes.

1 can (20 ounces) pineapple chunks packed without added sweetener
¼ cup apple cider vinegar
2 tablespoons honey
2 tablespoons arrowroot or cornstarch

1 tablespoon Tamari soy sauce
2½ cups cooked turkey, diced
1 green pepper cut into 1½-inch strips
1 small onion, thinly sliced
hot cooked brown rice or baked potatoes

Drain the pineapple, reserving the juice. Combine one cup of the pineapple juice with the vinegar, honey, arrowroot or cornstarch, and soy sauce. Cook over low heat until thickened, stirring constantly. Remove from the heat and add the turkey. Let stand, covered, for 10 minutes.

Place the green pepper strips in a little boiling water and cover. Let stand for 5 minutes. Drain well. Add the green pepper, onion, and pineapple chunks to the turkey mixture and heat. Season to taste.

Yield: 6 servings. *Each serving with ½ cup brown rice or 1 medium-size baked potato provides: approximately 179 cal, 18 g pro, 1.26 g sat fat, 2.52 g unsat fat, 66 mg chol, 162.5 mg sodium.*

Turkey and Broccoli Frittata

This is an adaptation of an omelet we very much enjoyed in Italy. Uncommonly good for a weekend family breakfast, lunch, or brunch, or for a patio dinner. Served this way, even George Bush Senior would eat his broccoli and love it.

3 tablespoons olive oil, chicken fat, or a combination of both

1 medium-size yellow onion, finely chopped

1 large clove garlic, minced

¾ cup cooked turkey, chopped

2 cups broccoli florets, chopped

½ cup cooked brown rice or pasta (optional)

6 eggs

2 teaspoons chopped fresh oregano or ½ teaspoon dried

½ teaspoon red pepper flakes, crushed

(continued)

Heat 2 tablespoons of the olive oil or chicken fat in a heavy, 10-inch skillet. Add the onion and sauté, stirring, until the onion is wilted and golden—about 6 minutes. Add the garlic and turkey and cook, stirring, for about 4 minutes. Stir in the broccoli and rice or pasta, if you're using it, and toss. Remove from the heat and set aside.

In a large bowl, food processor, or mixing machine, whisk the eggs until they are frothy. Add the turkey mixture and the oregano to the eggs.

Over moderate heat, add the remaining oil or fat to the skillet. Add the egg mixture, reduce the heat to low, and cook until the eggs are firm and brown on the underside—about 8 to 10 minutes. Sprinkle the red pepper flakes over the top, then run it under the broiler for about 4 minutes. Cut in wedges and serve from the skillet.

Yield: 6 servings. *Each serving provides: 210 cal, 15 g pro, 3.1 g sat fat, 8.1 g unsat fat, 316 mg chol, 100 mg sodium.*

12

MARVELOUS CHICKEN LIVER DISHES

If you've been enjoying chicken frequently, you probably have a goodly store of chicken livers in the freezer. Now's your chance to put them to good use and enhance the menu for a lovely family meal or for a very special occasion. Liver is the most nutritious of meats, especially rich in iron, vitamin A, and the B vitamins, including folic acid, which is important to everyone's health but especially important to women contemplating pregnancy. Well-documented research reveals that a deficiency of folic acid in the mother is responsible for such birth defects as spina bifida and cleft palate.

True, liver is high in cholesterol, but it has practically no saturated fat. Research points to saturated fat as the prime instigator of high cholesterol levels.

If, however, your doctor has restricted your cholesterol intake, enjoy chicken livers once in a while and limit your intake of other sources of high cholesterol foods on those occasions.

Curried Chicken Livers with Apples

Chicken livers go with chicken fat like love and marriage. If you don't have any chicken fat, use chicken broth.

1 pound chicken livers
1 teaspoon chicken fat (no substitutes)
½ cup chopped onions
¼ teaspoon curry powder
1 unpeeled apple (preferably Granny Smith), coarsely chopped
¼ cup raisins

2 tablespoons marsala wine
1 teaspoon arrowroot or cornstarch
2 tablespoons water
1 teaspoon no-salt herbal seasoning
¼ teaspoon freshly grated pepper

Cut the livers in halves and broil them 6 inches from the source of heat for 5 minutes on each side.

Heat the chicken fat in a heavy skillet. Add the onions, and sauté till tender. Stir in the chicken livers and curry powder. Add the apple and raisins, cover, and simmer for 10 minutes. Stir in the wine. Dissolve the arrowroot or cornstarch in the water and add to the mixture. Heat until slightly thickened. Add the seasonings.

Serve with hot cooked brown or wild rice, or a mixture of both. Garnish with thin apple slices and parsley or watercress.

Yield: 5 servings. *Each serving provides: 160 cal, 24 g pro, 1 g sat fat, 2 g unsat fat, 200 mg chol, 100 mg sodium.*

Chicken Liver Pâté with Toasted Almonds

1 tablespoon chicken fat
3 tablespoons chopped onion
½ pound chicken livers
2 tablespoons vermouth
1 hard-cooked egg
1 teaspoon herbal seasoning

¼ teaspoon freshly ground
   pepper
dash of nutmeg
½ cup toasted almonds,
   chopped
chicken broth

In a small skillet, heat the fat and sauté the onion. Set aside.

Broil the chicken livers for 5 minutes on each side.

Whir together in a food processor or chop in a wooden bowl the sautéed onions, livers, vermouth, egg, herbal seasoning, pepper, and nutmeg. Add a little chicken broth if necessary to make the pâté smoother. Fold in the chopped almonds. Refrigerate until ready to serve.

Yield: 2½ cups. *Each ¼-cup serving provides: 90 cal, 5 g pro, 1.8 g sat fat, 3.2 g unsat fat, 105 mg chol, 13 mg sodium.*

Variation: Instead of chopped almonds, fold in chopped chicken cracklings.

Oriental-Style Chicken Livers and Rice

1 cup uncooked brown rice
2½ cups chicken broth
1 pound chicken livers, cut in halves
2 tablespoons minced onion
2 tablespoons chopped green pepper
2 tablespoons chicken fat or olive oil, or a mixture
2 tablespoons reduced-sodium soy sauce
¼ teaspoon ground ginger

In a large saucepan, combine the rice and chicken broth. Bring to a boil, cover, and simmer for 35 minutes or until the liquid is absorbed and the rice is tender.

Broil the chicken livers for 3 minutes on each side.

In a heavy skillet, heat the chicken fat or olive oil. Brown the chicken livers, onion, and pepper. Stir in the soy sauce and ginger.

Spoon the rice onto a serving platter. Place the chicken livers in the center.

Yield: 4 servings. *Each serving provides: 388 cal, 29 g pro, 3.9 g sat fat, 7 g unsat fat, 402 mg chol, 610 mg sodium.*

Chopped Chicken Liver

This is the kind that Mamma used to make. For a special taste of nostalgia, serve it with grated white radish.

1 to 2 tablespoons chicken fat
¾ pound chicken livers (about 7 livers)
1 large onion, chopped fine
½ cup diced celery (optional)
1 hard-cooked egg
½ cup chicken cracklings (grieben)
1 large romaine leaf
1 teaspoon herbal seasoning
½ teaspoon freshly ground pepper, or to taste
sprig of parsley

In a large, heavy skillet, heat the fat and add the livers and onion, and the celery if you're using it. Sauté until the livers are firm but not overdone.

Combine the contents of the skillet with the hard-cooked egg, cracklings, and the romaine leaf. Put everything through a food chopper, or chop in a wooden bowl to a fine consistency but a slightly coarse texture. Add seasonings to taste. Shape the mixture into a neat mound and refrigerate. Serve cold, garnished with a sprig of parsley.

Yield: About 3 cups. *Each ¼-cup serving provides: 90 cal, 5 g pro, 1 g sat fat, 1.5 g unsat fat, 109 mg chol, 60 mg sodium.*

Chicken Livers and Spinach with Pistachios

This dish is a powerhouse of antifatigue iron, folic acid, and B$_{12}$, plus a big bunch of vitamin A, which perks up the immune system and has been shown to increase resistance to malignancies. Serve it with fiber-rich brown rice and apple sauce.

1 pound spinach, trimmed and washed
1 pound chicken livers

1 cup chicken broth
3 tablespoons shelled and chopped pistachios

In a dry saucepan, cook the spinach over medium heat for 2 minutes or just until wilted. Remove and leave to cool.

Broil the chicken livers for 2 minutes on each side. Mince the chicken livers with a knife or poultry shears.

Chop the cooked spinach and combine it with the chicken livers. Moisten with the chicken broth. Pack this combination into a baking dish greased with a little oil or sprayed with no-stick baking spray. Top with the chopped pistachios and bake in a preheated 350°F oven for about 30 minutes.

Yield: 4 servings. *Each serving provides: 185 cal, 28 g pro, 1.5 g sat fat, 2.5 g unsat fat, 250 mg chol, 92 mg sodium.*

Chicken Liver Soufflé

2 tablespoons plus 1 teaspoon
  chicken fat or olive oil
1 small onion, minced
3 tablespoons whole wheat
  flour
3 tablespoons oat bran
¼ teaspoon freshly ground
  pepper

¾ cup chicken broth
5 chicken livers
2 cloves garlic, minced
1 teaspoon finely minced
  fresh sage
3 tablespoons finely minced
  fresh parsley
4 eggs, separated

In a small skillet, heat 1 teaspoon chicken fat or olive oil. Add the onion and sauté until it is wilted and golden, about 8 minutes.

In a 2-quart saucepan, heat 2 tablespoons of fat. Add the flour, oat bran, and pepper, and stir with a wire whisk, cooking until bubbly but not brown. Whisk in the chicken broth gradually and cook slowly, stirring constantly until very thick, about 5 minutes. Remove from the heat and add the sautéed onions. Set aside to cool.

Broil the livers for 2 minutes on each side. In a food processor, food mill, or wooden bowl, blend the livers, garlic, sage, and parsley until smooth. Add this mixture to the sauce, then add the beaten egg yolks.

Coat a 2½-inch-deep soufflé dish with nonstick baking spray. Preheat the oven to 325°F.

In a medium-size bowl, beat the egg whites until stiff peaks form. Fold the whites into the liver mixture carefully. Spoon into the prepared soufflé dish and bake in the heated oven for 50 minutes or

(continued)

until a cake tester inserted in the center comes out clean. Serve at once before it deflates.

Yield: 6 servings. *Each serving provides: 151 cal, 10 g pro, 4 g sat fat, 5 g unsat fat, 215 mg chol, 200 mg sodium.*

Stewed Chicken Livers, Gizzards, and Hearts

A hearty, warming, nourishing dish. Serve with fiber-rich barley or buckwheat groats (kasha).

2 cups chicken stock
½ cup coarsely chopped onions
1 bay leaf
¼ teaspoon freshly ground pepper
¼ pound chicken hearts (optional)
½ pound chicken gizzards, cut in half
1 pound chicken livers, cut in bite-size pieces

6 tablespoons oat bran, for dredging
2 tablespoons chicken fat or olive oil
2 cloves garlic, finely minced
1 cup thinly sliced mushrooms
3 stalks celery, chopped
3 carrots, finely chopped
1 tablespoon fresh basil, minced
1 tablespoon fresh thyme leaves

In a large, heavy pot, combine the chicken stock, onions, bay leaf, pepper, chicken gizzards, and chicken hearts, if you're using them. Bring to a boil, cover, and simmer for 45 minutes or until the gizzards are tender. Remove and discard the bay leaf. With a slotted spoon, lift out the gizzards and hearts. Reserve the stock.

Cut the livers in halves, then broil them 2 minutes on each side. Dredge the livers in the oat bran. In a large skillet, heat the chicken fat or olive oil. Add the livers and sauté for 1 minute on each side. Lift out with a slotted spoon and reserve.

In the same skillet, add the garlic and mushrooms and stir for about 2 minutes over medium heat. Stir in the celery and carrots and cook for 2 more minutes. Add the reserved stock, gizzards, and hearts to the vegetables. Bring to a boil, cover, lower the heat, and simmer for about 12 minutes. Add the reserved livers, basil, and thyme, and heat, stirring occasionally until the sauce is thickened—about 5 minutes.

Yield: 6 servings. *Each serving provides: 204 cal, 22.2 g pro, 3 g sat fat, 4 g unsat fat, 319 mg chol, 210 mg sodium.*

Grilled Chicken Livers with Mushrooms

A tender, crunchy, epicurean delight—it beats hot dogs for an outdoor cookout.

1 pound chicken livers
1 tablespoon chicken fat or
    olive oil
¼ cup dry white wine
½ cup crushed oat bran
    crunch or your favorite
    high-fiber dry cereal

¼ teaspoon onion powder
¼ teaspoon dried oregano
8 medium-size mushrooms,
    halved, or 16 small
    mushrooms
8 cherry tomatoes

Cut the chicken livers in halves. Combine 1 tablespoon of chicken fat or olive oil and wine in a medium-size bowl and add the chicken livers. Marinate for 30 minutes, refrigerated.

On waxed paper, combine the cereal crumbs, onion powder, and oregano. Drain the chicken livers, reserving the marinade, and roll in the crumb mixture.

Thread the livers, mushrooms, and tomatoes alternately on 4 skewers. Brush with the reserved marinade.

Grill 15 minutes, turning once or until the livers are slightly browned.

Yield: 4 servings. *Each serving provides: 191 cal, 24 g pro, 2 g sat fat, 3 g unsat fat, 402 mg chol, 82 mg sodium.*

13

SPEEDY STIR-FRY DISHES

Stir-fry dishes can be very low in calories, highly nutritious, and exciting to make. A stir-fry always gets my creative juices flowing. There are so many different vegetables, grains, nuts, or seeds that can be added to a stir-fry, so many different herbs and condiments to mellow or sharpen flavors, so many nutritional dynamos you can add (or conceal, if you have a typically recalcitrant family), such as oat bran, rice bran, oatmeal, and all the veggies your family members think they don't like.

If you're on a tight schedule and must get dinner on the table in 15 minutes, prepare the vegetables when you do have time, blanche and freeze them in family-size packets, or use frozen vegetables.

Stir-fry dishes are quite flexible. They may be made from freshly cooked or leftover cooked poultry.

Another stir-fry virtue: a wonderful opportunity to use up all the odds and ends cluttering the refrigerator.

Skinny Ginger Garlic Chicken

Mushrooms and peppers are low-calorie pepper-uppers in this flavorful quick-and-easy dish.

1 chicken breast, boned and
   skinned (reserve the skin)
1 clove garlic, minced
1 slice ginger, minced
1 large red pepper, cut in
   wedges and sliced
1 large green or yellow
   pepper, cut in wedges
   and sliced

12 mushrooms, cleaned and
   sliced
4 water chestnuts, sliced
1 cup chicken broth
2 tablespoons reduced-sodium
   soy sauce
3 tablespoons sherry
½ teaspoon honey
2 cups cooked brown rice

Cut the breast in thin slices. Cut the skin in smallish pieces and render it in a heavy skillet or a wok. Remove the golden cracklings and reserve for another use. If the remaining fat is less than 2 tablespoons, add a little olive oil.

In the heated fat, lightly sauté the garlic and ginger for about a minute. Stir in the sliced chicken and cook for another minute. Add the peppers, mushrooms, and water chestnuts and cook until the chicken is cooked through.

Add the chicken broth, soy sauce, sherry, and honey and heat to combine the flavors. Serve over the brown rice or as a topping for baked potatoes.

Yield: 4 servings. *Each serving with ½ cup of brown rice provides: 177 cal, 13.5 g pro, 1.5 g sat fat, 3.12 g unsat fat, 66 mg chol, 328 mg sodium.*

Israeli-Style Chicken Curry

Intensify the Israeli experience and serve with a crisp potato kugel and pineapple cole slaw.

2 whole chicken breasts, boned and skinned (reserve the skin)
2 teaspoons dry sherry
2 teaspoons arrowroot or cornstarch
1 clove garlic, crushed
1 teaspoon curry powder
1 teaspoon herbal seasoning
1 cup Chinese pea pods
1 tomato, cut in 8 wedges
¼ cup chicken broth

Cut the chicken breasts into strips about ½ inch wide. Marinate in the sherry mixed with the arrowroot or cornstarch for 30 minutes or longer.

Render the chicken skin to make chicken fat. Retain 2 teaspoons of the fat, or use 2 teaspoons of olive oil.

In a large, heavy skillet or a wok, heat the fat and brown the garlic. Add the chicken and cook quickly until it turns white. Sprinkle with the curry powder and herbal seasoning.

Remove the chicken from the pan. In the same pan stir-fry the pea pods and tomatoes until heated through. Return the chicken to the pan with the vegetables. Add the chicken broth and cook until heated through.

Yield: 4 servings. *Each serving provides: 154 cal, 20.2 g pro, 0.5 g sat fat, 1.56 g unsat fat, 33 mg chol, 185 mg sodium.*

Chicken Chow Mein

Serve with brown rice. Pass the Chinese noodles and the chopsticks.

2 tablespoons olive oil or
    chicken fat or a
    combination
3 cups cooked chicken, cut in
    bite-size pieces
3 cups onions, sliced and then
    cut in half-moons
3 cups celery, sliced
    diagonally

3 cups chicken broth
2 cups bean sprouts
2 tablespoons arrowroot or
    cornstarch
2 tablespoons water
2 teaspoons reduced-sodium
    soy sauce
1 teaspoon honey

In a large skillet or a wok, heat the fat. Add the cut-up chicken. Sear it quickly without browning. Add the onions, and sauté for 3 minutes. Add the celery and chicken broth. Cook for 5 minutes or until the celery is slightly softened. Add the bean sprouts. Mix thoroughly and bring to a boil. Combine the arrowroot or cornstarch, water, soy sauce, and honey. Add to the chicken mixture. Cook 5 more minutes or until the sauce is slightly thickened.

Yield: 6 servings. *Each serving provides: 211 cal, 37 g pro, 1.2 g sat fat, 4.3 g unsat fat, 66 mg chol, 240 mg sodium.*

Orange Chicken and Bean Stir-fry

Beans provide not only incomparable flavor, they are also rich in water-soluble fiber, the kind that has been shown to lower high cholesterol levels. In addition, they are rich in blood-building iron. The vitamin C in the orange helps you to absorb the iron in the beans and in the chicken.

2 chicken breasts, boned and skinned (reserve skin)	2 medium green peppers, cut in ¼-inch pieces
½ cup orange juice	1 medium yellow onion, cut in ¼-inch slices
1½ teaspoons chili powder	
1½ teaspoons arrowroot or cornstarch	2 cups cooked or canned red kidney beans, drained
1 teaspoon herbal seasoning	2 medium tomatoes, cut in 8 wedges each

Cut the breasts crosswise in ⅛-inch slices.

In a shallow bowl, combine the orange juice, chili powder, arrowroot or cornstarch, and herbal seasoning. Add the chicken, stirring to mix. Set aside.

In a large skillet or a wok, render the skin of the chicken. Remove the cracklings and reserve. If you get less than 2 tablespoons of fat, add enough oil to make up the difference. Heat the fat to a high temperature, then add the peppers and onion and stir-fry about 4 minutes or just until the vegetables are crisp-tender.

Remove the vegetables and add the chicken to the drippings in the same skillet, but reserve the orange juice mixture.

(continued)

139

Cook the chicken, stirring constantly, for about 5 minutes or until golden. Add the reserved orange mixture, sautéed onions and peppers, kidney beans, and tomato wedges. Cook, stirring until heated through.

Yield: 6 servings. *Each serving provides: 228 cal, 23 g pro, 2.5 g sat fat, 4 g unsat fat, 70 mg chol, 60 mg sodium.*

Chicken Chop Suey with Brandy Sauce

Although this recipe calls for raw chicken, it can also be made from previously cooked chicken. It's delicious either way. The vegetables provide heart-healthy magnesium and potassium as well as beta-carotene, which has been shown to retard the development of carcinomas.

2 tablespoons olive, peanut, or canola oil
2 cups raw chicken, cut in 1-inch pieces
1 cup chicken broth
1 cup celery, cut in 1-inch chunks

12 water chestnuts, sliced (available in cans, or fresh at Oriental stores)
1 cup sliced, fresh mushrooms
1 cup sliced bamboo shoots or celery cabbage
1 cup bean sprouts
1 teaspoon herbal seasoning

BRANDY SAUCE

  1 tablespoon reduced-sodium   ½ teaspoon honey
       soy sauce   ½ jigger brandy
1½ teaspoons arrowroot or   ½ cup water
       cornstarch

In a large skillet or a wok, heat the oil. Add the chicken pieces and
cook until brown. Add the broth and remaining ingredients. Cover
and cook for 15 minutes, then add the sauce.

TO MAKE THE SAUCE: In a small bowl, combine all the ingredients
and mix until the sauce is thickened.

Yield: 4 servings. *Each serving provides: 218.5 cal, 15.7 g pro, 2.6 g sat
fat, 8.3 g unsat fat, 66 mg chol, 241 mg sodium.*

14

CHICKEN ON THE GRILL

To cook on a rack over hot coals, to invite the neighbors for a lovely picnic, to cause tantalizing aromas to invade the backyard, to obliterate all humdrum matters and stressful thoughts in anticipation of the joy of digging into a crisp-skinned, exquisitely flavored bird—that's grilling!

For the most delicious smoky flavor, start the barbecue about 40 minutes before you are ready to cook. The coals will then be grayed and burning at an even heat.

Recipes for broiled chicken can be grilled and vice versa. But bear in mind that charcoal broiling produces a higher direct heat, so cooking time will be shorter.

Marinades, commonly used on grilled chicken, contribute to a flavorsome moistness and tenderness. Marinades contain oil, an acid ingredient—vinegar or juice—for tenderizing, and seasonings for flavor.

When you grill kabobs over charcoal, place skewers on the barbecue rack, about 4 inches from coals, and turn the skewers frequently for even cooking.

To prevent dripping onto coals and causing flaming and smoking, remove the skewer from the barbecue grill when brushing it with marinade.

Orange Teriyaki Chicken

A spicy flavor zipped up with orange juice, which contributes valuable vitamin C, thus enhancing the utilization of the important minerals in all the ingredients.

¼ cup reduced-sodium soy
  sauce
3 tablespoons chopped onion
2 cloves garlic, minced
1 tablespoon olive or canola
  oil
½ teaspoon freshly ground
  pepper

½ teaspoon ground ginger
½ teaspoon Tabasco sauce
1 can (6-ounce) orange juice
  concentrate
2 broiler-fryers (2 to 2 ½
  pounds each), cut in
  serving pieces

In a bowl, combine all the ingredients except the chickens. Place the chicken pieces in a large bowl. Pour the orange juice marinade over the chicken. Marinate at least 3 hours, turning once, in the refrigerator.

Grill 4 to 6 inches from the heat source for 35 to 40 minutes, turning and basting with the marinade frequently.

Yield: 8 servings. *Each serving provides: 207 cal, 29 g pro, 1.5 g sat fat, 3.1 g unsat fat, 70 mg chol, 381 mg sodium.*

Honey-Glazed Chicken Kabobs with Sesame, Onions, and Squash

Squash contributes calcium, magnesium, potassium, and vitamin A, all important to healthy bones and the glow of health. Onions have been shown to lower harmful cholesterol levels. Both add flavor and gusto to this dish, which hints of the Orient.

2 tablespoons sesame seeds, lightly toasted
¼ cup honey
¼ cup lemon juice
1 teaspoon herbal seasoning
¼ teaspoon Tabasco sauce
8 small white onions, peeled and lightly steamed

2 small yellow squash, cut in 1-inch slices and lightly steamed
1 large red pepper, cut into 2-inch pieces
1 large green pepper, cut into 2-inch pieces
8 chicken thighs
¼ cup oil and vinegar salad dressing

In a bowl, combine the sesame seeds, honey, lemon juice, herbal seasoning, and Tabasco sauce.

Using 4 long skewers, thread the chicken thighs with the squash, onions, and peppers. Brush with the salad dressing.

Barbecue 4 inches from the coals for 10 minutes, turning several times. Brush with the sesame seed glaze, turning and basting for 10 minutes longer.

Yield: 4 servings. *Each serving provides: 351 cal, 33 g pro, 2 g sat fat, 7.3 g unsat fat, 70 mg chol, 260 mg sodium.*

Grilled Herb-Flavored Chicken Burgers

What's a cookout without burgers? Make yours with heart-healthy chicken. Enriched with oat bran and cornmeal, these burgers contribute valuable nutrients besides jolly enjoyment. Serve with sesame buns or whole wheat pits.

2 *cups skinless, boneless*
   chicken, cut in small cubes
¼ *cup chicken soup or stock*
1 *teaspoon herbal seasoning*
¼ *teaspoon freshly ground*
   pepper
2 *tablespoons finely chopped*
   fresh tarragon or
   1 teaspoon dried

½ *cup cornmeal*
½ *cup oat bran*
1 *tablespoon chicken fat or*
   olive oil
2 *teaspoons lemon juice*
2 *tablespoons chopped parsley*
¼ *teaspoon Tabasco® sauce*
   (optional)

In a chopping bowl or food processor, grind the chicken coarsely. Add the soup or stock, herbal seasoning, pepper, tarragon, cornmeal, and oat bran. Mix to combine the ingredients; do not overmix. The mixture should not be pasty.

Divide the mixture evenly into 8 patties. Dampen your hands and shape the portions into round, flat patties. Chill thoroughly for at least an hour before cooking.

Preheat the grill to high. Brush the surface with a little oil or coat with a nonstick baking spray. Grill the patties for about 4 minutes. Turn and grill for another 4 minutes.

(continued)

In a small skillet, heat the chicken fat or olive oil; add the lemon juice, parsley, and optional Tabasco® sauce; and pour over the patties. Serve at once.

Yield: 8 patties. *Each patty provides: 124 cal, 11.4 g pro, 1 g sat fat, 6.3 g unsat fat, 66 mg chol, 64 mg sodium.*

Grilled Chicken with Pine Nut or Walnut Pesto

The combination of basil and garlic generates a marvelous appetite-stimulating fragrance. If you have any leftover sauce, use it to flavor fish, pasta, or salad dressing.

2 cups loosely packed basil
   leaves
⅓ cup olive oil
⅓ cup pine nuts or walnut
   pieces, lightly toasted

2 cloves garlic, peeled
1 teaspoon herbal seasoning
3 chicken breasts, skinned,
   boned, and split

TO MAKE THE PESTO SAUCE: In a food processor fitted with a metal blade, combine the basil leaves and olive oil, pine nuts or walnut pieces, herbal seasoning, and garlic. Process until smooth. Transfer to a small bowl.

Brush the chicken breasts all over with the pesto sauce. Grill the breasts over hot coals, brushing occasionally with more sauce until cooked through, about 6 minutes on each side.

Pass the remaining sauce at the table, or reserve for another use.

Yield: 6 servings. *Each serving provides: approximately 337 cal, 26.5 g pro, 2 g sat fat, 13 g unsat fat, 66 mg chol, 150 mg sodium.*

15

LUSCIOUS, NUTRITIOUS STUFFINGS

Stuffings add an extra dimension of flavors, texture, and nutrients to the enjoyment of fowl. They can be made in infinite variety but tend to have a regional influence. In California they're into wild rice and mixed grains; in the Midwest stuffings are made with mushrooms, bread crumbs, and eggs; in New England they're usually made with chestnuts; and down South they're generally made with corn bread.

In the interests of food safety, many people opt to bake the stuffing as a casserole, where it develops a crisp crust.

If you prefer to put the stuffing in the bird, there are safety rules to heed.

According to the Turkey Talk-Line, the turkey, should be stuffed immediately before you put it in the oven, and the oven should be at least 350 degrees. The stuffing must be cooled before it is placed inside the bird and should be removed immediately after it is roasted. These measures retard spoilage.

Figure 1 cup of stuffing per pound of turkey.

A 13- to 15-pound turkey when stuffed should serve 24 people generously.

Pack the stuffing in with a light hand. Do not compress it, or it will be dense. Remember, it will expand during roasting.

Stuffings can be overly rich and outrageously caloric. They don't have to be. In the accompanying recipes I have reduced the fat, and with the addition of healthful grains and fruits enhanced the textures and flavors.

Basic Bread Stuffing

This is the traditional stuffing you probably remember so fondly, the way Mamma used to make it—but with a difference. This one is kind to your heart. The oat bran is a soluble fiber that lowers harmful cholesterol. The lecithin acts as an emulsifier that aids in the digestion of fats and breaks up cholesterol, helping to prevent atherosclerosis. The whole-grain bread and the wheat germ provide the B vitamins that fuel your energy pump and put a sparkle in your eye.

4 cups whole-grain bread
    cubes, lightly toasted
2 tablespoons poultry fat or
    olive, canola, or peanut
    oil
1 cup chopped onions
1 clove garlic, minced
1 cup chopped celery,
    including leaves
¼ cup wheat germ
¼ cup oat bran

2 tablespoons lecithin
    granules
½ teaspoon paprika
½ teaspoon ground sage
1 teaspoon freshly ground
    pepper
1 teaspoon dried thyme
2 eggs, beaten
½ cup chicken broth plus
    another ½ cup if stuffing
    is not cooked in bird

Place the bread cubes in a large bowl.

In a large skillet, heat the fat. Add the onions, garlic, and celery, and sauté until the onions are translucent. If it seems to need more fat, add a little chicken stock. Add this mixture to the bread cubes. Add the wheat germ, oat bran, lecithin granules, paprika, sage, pepper, thyme, and eggs. Toss. Add enough chicken broth to moisten the ingredients. Use to stuff poultry or add a little more broth, and bake in a greased baking dish at 325°F for 45 to 60 minutes or until lightly browned.

Yield: About 8 cups or 16 servings. *Each serving provides: 95 cal, 19 g pro, 0.5 g sat fat, 2.2 g unsat fat, 30 mg chol, 123 mg sodium.*

Almond, Apple, and Bulgur Stuffing

A lovely combination of fruit, nuts, and grains. This makes a delicious casserole for a fish dinner when you don't have a bird to stuff.

2 tablespoons poultry fat or olive, canola, or peanut oil	1 cup bulgur
	3 cups diced apples
	½ cup chopped almonds
1 large clove garlic, minced	½ teaspoon ground nutmeg
1 cup chopped onions	¼ teaspoon allspice
1 cup chopped celery	½ teaspoon freshly ground
4 cups poultry stock or water	pepper

In a medium-size saucepan, heat the fat or oil. Add the garlic, onions, and celery and sauté till the onions are wilted. Add the poultry stock

(continued)

or water. Stir in the bulgur. Bring to a boil, reduce the heat, then simmer, covered, for about 30 minutes.

Add the apples, almonds, and spices to the bulgur and mix well.

Yield: About 5 cups or 10 servings. *Each serving provides: 171 cal, 5 g pro, 0.7 g sat fat, 6.2 unsat fat, no chol, 31 mg sodium.*

Susie's Corn Bread Stuffing

If you're from down South, you probably call it "dressing" and you wouldn't think of stuffing the bird with anything else.

3 tablespoons poultry fat or
   olive, canola, or peanut
   oil, or a combination
1 medium-size onion,
   chopped
1 large red bell pepper,
   chopped
2 ribs celery with leaves,
   chopped
¼ cup chopped parsley
2 scallions, chopped
6 cups 3-day-old corn bread,
   crumbled
1 cup oat bran crunch,
   crushed

½ cup wheat germ
2 tablespoons lecithin
   granules
⅓ cup chopped nuts (any
   kind, or a mixture of
   nuts and sunflower
   seeds)
1 tablespoon vegetable
   seasoning, or to taste
1 teaspoon freshly ground
   pepper
½ teaspoon sage
½ teaspoon Tabasco® sauce
1 cup chicken broth if stuffing
   is baked in a casserole

In a large skillet, heat the fat or oil. Add the onion and sauté until it is wilted, about 5 minutes. Add the red bell pepper and celery and cook another 5 minutes.

Place the onion mixture in a large bowl. Add the parsley, scallions, corn bread, oat bran crunch, wheat germ, lecithin granules, nuts, vegetable seasoning, pepper, Tabasco® and sage. Stir to combine. When cool, fill the turkey with this mixture, being careful not to pack it. Leave room for expansion. Or, if you prefer, place the stuffing in a greased casserole and bake at 350°F for 40 minutes.

Yield: About 8 cups or 16 servings. *Each serving provides: 126 cal, 5 g pro, 0.4 g sat fat, 3.8 g unsat fat, no chol, 110 mg sodium.*

Spicy Aromatic Rice Stuffing

Here's the intriguing flavor of the Orient enriched with brown rice, a good source of water-soluble rice bran, which, like oat bran, tends to lower harmful cholesterol levels.

2 cups chicken stock or water,
    or a combination
1 cup brown rice
2 tablespoons chicken fat or
    olive, canola, or peanut
    oil, or a combination
2 large onions, sliced
1 large garlic clove, minced
2 cups sliced mushrooms
½ cup raisins

2 teaspoons minced fresh
    ginger
¼ teaspoon ground cardamom
¼ teaspoon cinnamon
¼ teaspoon freshly ground
    pepper
⅛ teaspoon ground cloves
½ cup unsalted cashews,
    lightly roasted, coarsely
    chopped

In a medium saucepan, combine the stock or water and rice and bring to a boil. Reduce the heat, cover, and simmer until the rice is tender and the stock or water is absorbed—about 40 minutes.

In a large skillet, heat the chicken fat or oil. Add the onions and garlic, cover, and cook, stirring occasionally, until the onions are translucent—about 8 minutes. Add the mushrooms, raisins, ginger, and spices, and cook for about 5 minutes, or until the mushrooms are soft. Remove from the heat. Stir in the cooked rice and the cashews.

Refrigerate before using.

Yield: About 7 cups or 14 servings. *Each serving provides: 96 cal, 3.5 g pro, 0.4 g sat fat, 2.8 g unsat fat, no chol, 42 mg sodium.*

David's Chestnut Stuffing

Irresistibly good, the favored stuffing in New England—and a wise choice. Chestnuts bring a rich, nutty flavor, and yet they are very low in fat, only 1.5 grams per 100 grams as compared to almonds, which have 54 grams per 100 grams. The prunes are a flavorful counterpoint and provide lots of potassium, blood-building iron, and immunity-enhancing vitamin A.

1 pound chestnuts
2 cups pitted prunes
   hot herbal tea to cover
    prunes
1 turkey gizzard, trimmed of
   tough membranes
1 turkey liver
1 teaspoon poultry fat or
   olive, canola, or peanut
   oil
1 teaspoon ground sage
1 teaspoon rosemary

1 teaspoon herbal seasoning
½ teaspoon freshly ground
   pepper
2 pears, washed, cored, and
   cut into small cubes
3 apples, washed, cored, and
   cut into small cubes
½ cup coarsely chopped
   pecans or walnuts,
   lightly toasted
½ cup cognac

Unless the chestnuts are purchased already cooked, prepare them this way: With a sharp paring knife, make an incision around the perimeter of each chestnut. Place them in one layer in a baking dish. Bake in a preheated 450°F oven for 10 minutes or until they open. Let them cool until they can be handled, but peel them while they are hot. Cut them into ½-inch cubes.

(continued)

Place the prunes in a bowl and add the tea to cover. Let soak until ready to use.

Grind together the gizzard and the liver. In a small skillet, heat the poultry fat or oil, and cook the liver mixture until it loses its raw, red color. Place this mixture into a bowl. Add the sage, rosemary, herbal seasoning, and pepper.

Drain the prunes and cut them into smallish pieces. Add them to the liver mixture. Add the chestnuts, pears, apples, nuts, and cognac. Blend well. Stuff a 10- to 12-pound turkey. Do not compress or pack the stuffing. If there is an excess of stuffing, place it in a small greased baking dish and bake along with the turkey for about 40 minutes.

Yield: About 8 cups or 16 servings. *Each serving provides: 132 cal, 3 g pro, tr sat fat, 2 g unsat fat, no chol, 15 mg sodium.*

Kasha Stuffing with Mushrooms, Apples, and Raisins

Kasha or buckwheat is a warming food. Maybe that's why it's so popular in Russia. Kasha, which is roasted buckwheat, is high in fiber and a good source of rutin, a bioflavonoid, important to the building and maintenance of cartilage and an important antioxidant, a food factor that enhances your resistance to the development of carcinomas.

2 tablespoons poultry fat or olive, canola, or peanut oil

2½ cups chopped onions

2 cups sliced mushrooms

2 cups cooked kasha (cooked in chicken stock)

3 tart apples, washed, cored, and cut in small cubes

½ cup raisins

½ teaspoon cinnamon

1 tablespoon sage

1 teaspoon herbal seasoning

½ teaspoon freshly ground pepper

2 tablespoons lecithin granules

In a skillet, heat the poultry fat or oil and sauté the onions over moderate heat for 5 minutes or until the onions are translucent. Add the mushrooms, increase the heat slightly, and sauté the mixture for 3 minutes. Transfer to a large bowl and add the kasha, apples, raisins, sage, herbal seasoning, cinnamon, lecithin granules, and pepper.

Yield: About 7 cups or 14 servings. *Each serving provides: 120 cal, 2.6 g pro, tr sat fat, 1.8 g unsat fat, no chol, 10 mg sodium.*

16

LOVELY COMPANIONS

What you serve as side dishes with your chicken dinner provide the grace notes to a veritable symphony of flavors and textures. I like to serve something tart and moist, like a fruity dish, and something in the complex carbohydrate family, like rice, potatoes, or pasta. Such accompaniments not only complement the nutrients in the chicken, providing vitamin C and fiber, they also make for a very pleasant and enjoyable dining experience.

The recipes that follow provide a whole palette of colors, flavors, and textures to choose from.

Cranberry Applesauce

This sauce, made without any sweetener, is sweet enough to double as a jam, should you have any left over.

1 pound fresh cranberries
1 cup apple cider or apple juice
½ teaspoon cinnamon
9 small red apples, scrubbed, cored, and chopped
½ cup currants or raisins
1 tablespoon orange juice
2 teaspoons grated orange rind

Rinse and sort the cranberries.

In a large, heavy saucepan, bring the apple cider or apple juice to a boil. Add the cinnamon and cranberries. Boil until the cranberries begin to pop. Add the apples, currants or raisins, orange juice, and orange rind. Cover and simmer for 20 minutes. Purée the sauce in a blender or food processor if desired.

Yield: 7 cups or 14 servings. *Each ½-cup serving provides: 74 cal, no fat, no chol, 2 mg sodium.*

Candied Sweet Potatoes

These have all the irresistible appeal of the usual candied sweet potatoes, but without added sweeteners. Each sweet potato provides as much as 11,610 units of beta-carotene, the nutrient that has been shown to retard the development of cancer. Sweet potatoes also provide potassium, calcium, and marvelous flavor.

6 good-size sweet potatoes
4 tablespoons fruit juice-
sweetened apricot
preserves or orange
marmalade

Bake or steam the sweet potatoes until soft. Split and place face up in a baking pan. Spread a teaspoon of preserves over each half. Place under the broiler for a few minutes, until the top is bubbly.

Yield: 12 servings. *Each serving provides: 85 cal, 1 g pro, no sat fat, 0.25 g unsat fat, no chol, 6 mg sodium.*

Potato Knishes

At our house, a supply of knishes in the freezer is better than money in the bank. They make any meal special and are a must for holiday meals. Our kids call these knishes "convertibles" because they don't have hard tops like knishes that are rolled in dough. These are much easier to make and very tasty. Potatoes are high in vitamin C complex, a better vitamin C pattern than is found in citrus fruit because it contains the tyrosinase fraction, an organic copper blood-builder. Potatoes also provide potassium, magnesium, calcium, and iron.

6 *large potatoes, steamed in their jackets, then peeled and mashed*
2 *eggs, beaten (reserve 2 tablespoons)*
grieben (chicken cracklings), as many as you can spare, chopped

1 *onion, chopped and sautéed in 1 teaspoon chicken fat (if you don't have any grieben, sauté 2 chopped onions in 2 teaspoons chicken fat)*
salt or vegetable seasoner and pepper to taste

In a large mixing bowl, mix together the mashed potatoes, beaten eggs, grieben and/or sautéed onions, and salt or vegetable seasoner. Form into patties about ½-inch thick, 3 inches long, and 2 inches wide. Place on a cookie sheet coated with a no-fat cooking spray, or greased with a little chicken fat or oil. Brush the patties with the reserved egg. Bake in a preheated 375°F oven for about 35 minutes or until brown and fragrant.

Yield: 12 knishes. *Each knish provides: 60 cal, 2.5 g pro, tr sat fat, 1.2 g unsat fat, 41.6 mg chol, 10 mg sodium.*

Sweet Potato, Apple, and Granola Bake

An excellent side dish and exceptionally nutritious. Apples provide a sweet tartness and gobs of pectin, which has been shown to decrease cholesterol concentration significantly, not only in the blood but also in the liver. In addition, pectin tends to bind with many toxic elements and ushers them out of the body. Granola is rich in morale-boosting vitamin B and valuable fiber.

4 medium-size sweet potatoes
   or yams
3 medium-size apples
1 cup apple, orange, or
   pineapple juice
1 tablespoon arrowroot or
   cornstarch

2 tablespoons water
1 tablespoon honey
½ cup granola or wheat germ
   chopped nuts (optional)
   cinnamon

Steam the sweet potatoes or yams for 15 to 20 minutes or until tender. Peel and cut in ½-inch slices. Layer in a 9 x 9-inch ungreased casserole. Wash and core the apples. Slice about ¼-inch thick and layer on top of the sweet potatoes or yams.

In a saucepan, heat the fruit juice to a boil. Combine the arrowroot or cornstarch and water and add it to the juice, cooking until the sauce has thickened. Add the honey and stir. Pour the sauce over the sliced apples, then top with granola or wheat germ. If using wheat germ, add some chopped nuts. Dust with a little cinnamon. Bake in a preheated 325°F oven for 30 to 40 minutes or until the apple slices are tender.

Yield: 8 servings. *Each serving provides: 127 cal, 1.7 g pro, tr sat fat, 0.5 g unsat fat, no chol, 5 mg sodium.*

Noodle Kugel

Fantastic with chicken and so easy to prepare, this kugel is light as a soufflé and has a crunchy crust and a hearty flavor. Wheat germ and oat bran provide essential nutrients and fiber. Lecithin granules help keep cholesterol under control.

8 ounces fine noodles, cooked and drained
6 eggs, well beaten
2 tablespoons oat bran
½ cup wheat germ
2 tablespoons lecithin granules
2 teaspoons herbal seasoning
½ teaspoon freshly ground pepper
¼ teaspoon cinnamon
2 tablespoons chicken fat or olive, canola, or peanut oil
sesame seeds

In a large bowl combine the cooked noodles, oat bran, wheat germ, lecithin granules, herbal seasoning, pepper, and cinnamon. Mix well.

Heat 1 tablespoon of the chicken fat or oil in an 8 x 10-inch baking dish. Pour in the noodle mixture and top with sesame seeds. Drizzle the remaining chicken fat or oil on top. Bake in a preheated 400°F oven for 35 minutes or until nicely browned.

Yield: 10 servings. *Each serving provides: 180 cal, 8.6 g pro, 1.8 g sat fat, 5 g unsat fat, 150 mg chol, 42.4 mg sodium.*

Potato Kugel

This crisp-crusted, moist, and savory kugel is a perfect partner for roast chicken or turkey and, in the food processor, can be made quick as a wink minus the scraped knuckles.

Potatoes are a good source of fiber, a good energy food, and low in calories. There are only 90 calories in a 5-ounce potato, which also provides 20 milligrams of vitamin C, as much as you would get in half a glass of tomato juice, as much protein as in half a cup of milk, and much more iron and niacin than in half a cup of milk. A real nutritional bargain.

3 *large unpeeled potatoes, scrubbed and cut in 8 large dice*
1 *medium-size onion, cut in large dice*
2 *tablespoons wheat germ*
2 *tablespoons oat bran*
2 *tablespoons lecithin granules*
⅛ *teaspoon freshly ground pepper or to taste*
2 *teaspoons herbal seasoning, or to taste*
    dash of cinnamon
3 *eggs*
2 *tablespoons chicken fat or olive, canola, or peanut oil*

In a bowl or food processor fitted with a steel blade, whiz the potatoes and onions until well grated but not puréed. Add the wheat germ, oat bran, lecithin granules, herbal seasoning, pepper, cinnamon, and eggs. Whiz to combine.

Heat 1 tablespoon of chicken fat or oil in a 9 x 9-inch baking dish. Add the potato mixture. Drizzle the other tablespoon of chicken fat or oil over the top. Bake in a preheated 350°F oven for about 1 hour or until brown and crisp. Serve with applesauce.

Yield: 8 servings. *Each serving provides: 125 cal, 4.3 g pro, 1.4 g sat fat, 2 g unsat fat, 94 mg chol, 8 mg sodium.*

Saffron Rice Salad

A warm-weather delight.

2 tablespoons wine or balsamic vinegar
1 teaspoon olive oil
1 clove garlic, minced
¼ teaspoon freshly ground pepper

2½ cups cooked brown rice, cooked in chicken broth, with ¹⁄₁₆ teaspoon saffron or ground turmeric
½ cup diced red pepper
½ cup diced green pepper
¼ cup sliced green onions
¼ cup sliced ripe olives

In a large salad bowl, combine the wine or vinegar, olive oil, garlic, and pepper. Mix well. Add the rice, red and green peppers, onions, and olives. Toss to combine the ingredients.

Yield: 5 servings. *Each serving provides: 116 cal, 2.6 g pro, 0.1 g sat fat, 1 g unsat fat, no chat, 223 mg sodium.*

Broccoli with Shredded Wheat Topping

Even your vegetable-scorners will go for this version. The crunchy topping contributes high-octane vitamin B's and lots of fiber. Broccoli, the darling of the vegetable bin, is a member of the cruciferous family, which has been shown to be an important ally in the fight against stomach and colon cancer.

1 bunch broccoli (about 1½ pounds), trimmed, cut in 1 ½-inch pieces, and steamed
1 teaspoon olive oil
⅓ cup chopped onion
1 clove garlic
½ cup crushed shredded wheat
½ teaspoon Worcestershire sauce

In a small skillet, heat the olive oil, add the onion and garlic, and sauté until golden, about 1 minute. Add the shredded wheat and Worcestershire sauce. Mix well. Place the cooked broccoli in a serving dish. Sprinkle with the shredded wheat topping. Place under the broiler for about 3 minutes, or in the microwave on high for 30 seconds.

Yield: 8 servings. *Each serving provides: 35 cal, 1.3 g pro, tr sat fat, 0.5 g unsat fat, no chol, 10 mg sodium.*

Part Two

Smart Fish

INTRODUCTION

Why Fish Is a Smart Food Choice

Fish has long enjoyed a reputation as a brain food, probably because of its high content of phosphorus, a mineral the brain likes to play around with.

Even though they spend most of their lives in schools, there is no hard evidence that eating fish will enhance your chances of winning at *Jeopardy*. But there is much evidence implying that you are smart to make fish a frequent part of your meal plan—if not for your brain, for your heart.

A VALENTINE FOR YOUR HEART . . .

Many studies have demonstrated that the special Omega-3 fatty acids in fish can:

- unclog arteries,

- lower levels of dangerous low-density cholesterol,

- lower levels of triglycerides, another group of blood fats that pose a threat to your heart,

- make the blood less prone to clotting,

- have a positive effect on cancer, diabetes, psoriasis, migraine headaches, arthritis, auto-immune diseases, and inflammatory diseases.

. . . AND YOUR FIGURE

Fish has its merits for everyone. But, for those who wish to cut calories without sacrificing nutrients, fish is definitely a top-of-the-barrel catch. At approximately 100 calories in three ounces, fish is an attractive alternative to the 330 calories in an equivalent amount of meat.

Compared to fish oil, a typical vegetable oil provides as many as 60 percent more calories in attaining the same degree of total polyunsaturation in the diet. That's because, while vegetable oil may contain two, but never more than three sites of unsaturation, fish oils have four, five, or even six sites of unsaturation, thus giving fish oils a much greater degree of polyunsaturation than vegetable oils.

Fish do vary in caloric content, according to the amount of fat they contain. Four ounces of raw haddock, cod, and flounder provide only 85 calories. The same amount of swordfish or bluefish contain about 135 calories. But, even mackerel—which tops the list at 220 calories in four ounces—contains substantially fewer calories than an equal amount of meat.

Not only will fish, prepared with a smart flair, delight you with its succulent goodness, it will provide your body with almost all the important nutrients: protein, vitamins, minerals, and trace elements.

The vitamin content of fish, as with all fresh foods, is subject to seasonal change. Vitamin A content is highest in summer, but remains very high in the winter months, as compared with other foodstuffs.

Strange as it may seem, fish is low in sodium. This goes for ocean fish as well as freshwater fish, and is one reason why fish is so frequently prescribed for patients with high blood pressure. Fish also provides lots of phosphorus, necessary to the brain, as I said earlier. Calcium, too, is found in fish in a form that is just as absorbable as that found in milk. In fact, the calcium-phosphorus proportion corresponds roughly to that of milk. But the very important and scarce mineral magnesium is higher in fish than it is in dairy products.

Fish also contributes to your iron stores. It is a common misconception that you must have red meat for good blood. Experiments have shown that, when seafoods are used as the main protein constituent of human diets, both red cell count and hemoglobin levels are maintained as well as with meat.

It is well known that fish are a marvelous source of iodine, so important to the thyroid gland. What is not so well known is that fish are an excellent source of copper, an essential mineral that is scarce in the usual fare, and that is necessary for making hemoglobin out of iron.

Fish certainly goes to the head of the class when it comes to "smart foods." But how you prepare that fish for the table can subtract from its nutritional score or can enhance it. Many fish recipes (not in this book) call for deep-fat frying or the addition of one or two tablespoons of butter. Not necessary.

In this book, we're playing it "smart." We have devised some highly pleasing recipes, rich in nutrients, and with added fiber—the one essential nutrient that fish leaves out of the swim. Try them. We think they will pleasure your palate, your waistline, and your well-being.

Seafood Safety—
What Are the Facts?

An article in *Consumer Reports* magazine published early in 1992, raising questions about the quality, wholesomeness, and safety of the fish we are eating, has sparked a flurry of concern.

And rightly so. We should be concerned. After all, most of us are eating more fish to reap the benefits of a low-fat diet and the high content of the health-protective Omega-3 fatty acids. So what are the facts? Smart consumers want to know.

Just as in a political campaign, there is another side to the fish-safety story. Now, hear this: The American Institute for Cancer Research newsletter reports that:

- A recent study by the National Academy of Sciences gave our seafood a clean bill of health.

- According to the Centers for Disease Control, seafood accounted for only 5 percent of all food-poisoning cases reported between 1973 and 1987.

- The U.S. Food and Drug Administration (FDA) reports that seafood-related illnesses are decreasing even as Americans eat more seafood.

- The FDA recently conducted a special inspection of all seafood-processing plants in the United States. Inspectors checked to be sure that plants met sanitation and foodhandling regulations, and they found violations in only a small percentage of cases.

- The FDA regularly analyzes seafood for pesticides and industrial chemicals. In 1992, it increased domestic sampling by 50 percent and doubled sampling of imports.

However, to eliminate even that small percentage of violations, many consumer organizations are backing legislation now before Congress designed to create a more comprehensive government system to regulate the seafood industry.

In the meantime, you don't have to limit your consumption of "smart fish." While bacteria can frequently be found on shellfish taken from waters tainted by raw sewage, fin fish normally are unaffected. All the recipes in this *Smart Fish* cookbook call for fin fish.

What to Look For
When You Buy Fish

If you, a family member, a friend, or a neighbor love to go fishing, you're in luck. Believe me, freshly caught fish, put on the grill the moment you dock your boat, is like a taste of heaven.

Lacking a home-grown fisherman, you might develop a friendly relationship with the person from whom you buy fish. Choose a reliable dealer on whom you can depend for top quality and honest judgment. Shop for clothes and accessories in a thrift shop if you're economizing, but never, never compromise on the quality of fish. Buy the best. The best is not necessarily the most expensive, but, most emphatically, insist on top quality.

Your nose and your eyes are your most important tools when you are looking for fresh, top-quality fish. If there is any odor at all, it should be mild and evoke the aroma of a fresh ocean breeze. Pass up any fish that smells *noticeably* fishy.

Top-quality fish looks as if it has just jumped out of the water. It should have a lustrous sheen and bright skin color. The eyes should be bright and full and never sunken. The gills should be reddish-pink, clean, and not sticky. The flesh of the fish should be firm, elastic, and moist. Scales should have a sheen and adhere tightly. When buying fillets, look for moist, glossy translucent flesh. Pass up fillets that are dry or slimy.

Buy fresh fish when it is in season in your locality. That's when it is best and is least expensive. Try less familiar varieties when they are abundant and inexpensive. The demand for favorite varieties frequently increases the price. As Georges Auguste Escoffier, the renowned French chef, pointed out years ago, "The culinary value of the fish has far less to do with the vogue it enjoys than the very often freakish whims of the public."

HOW MUCH SHOULD I BUY?

How much should you buy? As a general rule, figure six to eight ounces for each adult, a little less for children. Be sure to mentally calculate the weight of the fish after skin, bones, scales, etc., have been removed. Also, articulate clearly when ordering. I once asked for two pounds of bluefish fillet. What I got was a two-pound blue, filleted, which left me with only fourteen ounces of fish to feed four adults and one child.

Believe me, it's much better to have too much than too little. Leftover fish makes a great salad or tasty fish cakes.

MARKET FORMS

At the market, fish is available in these forms:

- Whole or round—fish as they come from the water

- Whole dressed—fish with scales, entrails, and usually the head, tail, and fins removed. Allow about three-quarters of a pound per person. Don't hesitate to ask for the head and carcass when you have a whole fish filleted. Use for stock. Be sure to eat the very tasty chunks of fish encased in the head. This was my Mom's favorite nosh. "It's what makes me so smart," she would say with a wink. When I order whole dressed fish, I specify that I want the head and the tail left on; this makes for a juicier, tastier dish. For squeamish eaters, remove the head before serving.

- Pan dressed—the term referring to smaller fish weighing about one pound, with head, tail, and fins removed—except for very small fish like smelt, which are usually sold whole. Allow a half pound per serving.

- Steaks—cross-section slices, about ⅝ to 1 inch thick, of large, firm-fleshed fish such as salmon, swordfish, halibut, and cod. One pound will serve two or three.

- Fillets—boneless sides of fish cut lengthwise away from the backbone and rib cage. One pound should serve three.

- Frozen fish—fish that is frozen stiff and has no signs of having been refrozen or of freezer burn. (Light-colored spots indicate freezer burn. This occurs when the fish is not packaged tightly.)

You know that fish has been thawed and refrozen when it is contorted in shape. Once a frozen fish is thawed, it must be cooked quickly. I like to remove frozen fish from the freezer about a half hour before cooking so that it will still be somewhat solid when it hits the heat. Granted that frozen fish is not so tasty as fresh fish, but it's better than no fish.

STORING

Because fish is so perishable, it is always displayed on ice but, if you're not going to cook it immediately, store it in your refrigerator on a bed of ice—for no more than 24 hours. This reduces the temperature, bringing it close to zero, but it doesn't freeze it.

If you plan to freeze your own catch, be sure to set the freezer at zero degrees. If freezer space is at a premium, remove head and bones and make stock. Fillet the fish and freeze it along with the stock.

Discover the Many Ways to Prepare Succulent Fish

If every time you think fish, you reach for the frying pan, you'll be amazed and delighted with the moist, flavorful fish you will bring to the table when you try other techniques such as:

STEAMING. In a covered pot, a wok, or a fish poacher, place the fish on a rack above a swirling liquid that may be water, wine, or flavored broth. This is an excellent method for preserving the delicate flavor of lean fish, either fillets or small whole fish. Figure one minute for each ounce of fish, but test early to prevent overcooking.

POACHING. This method differs from steaming in that the fish is completely immersed in an aromatic broth and simmered, not boiled, for about 6 to 8 minutes per pound. The fish should be wrapped in a double layer of moistened cheesecloth, allowing extra length at each end for easy removal.

BROILING. This is an excellent way to develop flavor in fatty fish, small fish left whole after dressing, fish cut into chunks, whole fish that are butterflied, and fillets and steaks. Fish to be broiled should range in thickness from ½ inch to 1½ inches. Thicker than 1½ inches would dry out before being fully cooked. (For thicker fish, baking is a more effective method.) To broil, place the fish on a perforated rack that fits over a pan. The rack should be oiled, buttered, or sprayed with non-stick cooking spray. Broil about 4 inches below the source of heat. Thick steaks and whole fish should be turned over with a wide spatula.

BAKING. Any and every kind of fish can be baked. This is the most expedient way to cook large, whole stuffed fish; but smaller fillets and steaks may also be baked. Place the fish in a baking dish that has been oiled, buttered, or sprayed with nonfat cooking spray, and bake, uncovered, in an oven preheated to 350–375 degrees. Test frequently to determine doneness.

FRYING. Pan-frying, oven-frying, and deep-frying are quick cooking methods that contribute a nice crunchy exterior, a moist interior, and lots of flavor. Choose small whole fish or fillets for frying. (The coating on thick pieces of fish tends to burn before the fish is cooked through.) To pan-fry fish, bread it lightly, then place it in a skillet with a thin layer of heated oil over medium heat and fry it briefly on both sides until golden brown.

Oven-fried fish is also lightly breaded, placed in a baking dish that has been oiled, buttered, or sprayed with a non-stick cooking spray and then placed in a hot oven (450 to 500 degrees). The fish cooks quickly and does not have to be turned.

Deep-fried fish, reminiscent of the Fish 'n Chips that was consumed in huge quantities in my New England hometown, is dipped in batter, then cooked in very hot oil (370 degrees) in a deep-frying pan until golden brown.

LEFTOVER FISH

I always prepare more fish than we can eat, in order to ensure there will be leftovers. We love it in cold salad with a tart dressing, or made into a seafood quiche. Sometimes I mix the fish with bread crumbs, wheat germ, some mashed potatoes, and seasonings, or bind the mixture with a beaten egg and fill the house with the appetizing aroma of sizzling fish cakes!

Microwaving Fish

Remember the Canadian rule of ten minutes cooking time for every inch of thickness of the fish? Forget it when you're microwaving. Fish in the microwave cooks in about half the time it takes in a conventional oven—about 4 minutes a pound on high or one minute for every 3½ ounces.

The recipes in this book that call for baking or poaching will do very well in the microwave and will be lower in calories because it is not necessary to add fat or to grease the casserole.

Because there is so little evaporation of liquids in the microwave, reduce the amount of liquid called for in the recipe by about one-third. Cover the fish with a damp paper towel, waxed paper, or microwave-safe plastic wrap. For added flavor, wrap the fish in romaine lettuce or, if you relish a slightly tart flavor, as I do, wrap the fish in fresh sorrel leaves.

When arranging the fish in the microwave-safe casserole, be sure to place the thinnest part in and the thickest part out, or overlap the thinner ends so that the fish is of uniform thickness.

If you're microwaving a whole fish, it's a good idea to cover the head and tail with aluminum foil to protect them from scorching and prevent the eyes from popping.

Microwave cooking calls for split-second timing. When the flesh begins to lose its translucence, remove it from the micro-oven and let it stand, covered, for a few minutes. It will then complete its cooking and be tender, flaky, and rich in good satisfying flavors.

17

APPETIZERS

Appetizers can be a prelude to the main meal, or, served in larger portions, can be the meal itself. Any savory dish can be served as an appetizer. Just serve it in small quantities or as a finger food, so that it piques the appetite but does not satisfy it. I especially like to serve fish appetizers when the main meal does not include fish. In this way I can assure that my family will be getting the important nutrients that only fish can provide.

In the following ten recipes I have put the emphasis on herring and sardines because these fish are under-utilized as main dishes, yet they provide many valuable nutrients. Sardines, for instance, which are really undersized herring, pack a whale of a lot of good nutrients into their tiny little bodies. Their protein content is high; they provide all the B vitamins except thiamine, with unusually high levels of folate and vitamin B_{12}. Sardines are one of the few food sources of vitamin D, the nutrient essential to the utilization of calcium. And because you consume the bones in these delicate little fish, you also get a good supply of calcium.

For those who wish to cut calories without sacrificing nutrients, sardines provide a tasty alternative to other sources of protein. Even when packed in oil, they contribute a modest 186 calories for an average serving. To further limit the calorie content, pour off the oil. Calories will drop to 122. To cut down on the sodium, rinse in cold water.

The recipes that follow will help you devise a tray of appetizers that tease the appetite. Bear in mind that with appetizers the presentation can also stimulate the appetite. Arrange them attractively on pretty trays. Consider texture and color to please the eye as well as the palate. Go creative with colorful garnishes: bright orange carrot curls, sprigs of green parsley or dill, ruby-red radish roses, green and red pepper rings, black and green olives, and sprigs of whatever fresh herbs are growing on your windowsill or in your garden—basil, thyme, oregano, mint, or chervil.

Mushrooms Stuffed with Tuna and Water Chestnuts

An enticing tidbit, these are easy to prepare and low in calories.

1 *pound fresh mushrooms (large ones preferable)*
1 *can tuna (6 ½ or 7 ounces) in oil, drained*
2 *teaspoons reduced-sodium soy sauce*

¼ *cup chopped water chestnuts (almonds may be substituted)*
½ *teaspoon powdered ginger*

Wipe the mushroom caps with a damp paper towel. Remove stems and reserve for another use. Place the mushroom caps, top side down, on a baking sheet that has been lightly greased or sprayed with a

(*continued*)

non-stick baking spray. In a small bowl, combine the remaining ingredients. Spoon this mixture into the mushroom caps. Bake, uncovered, at 350 degrees for 5 to 6 minutes, until steaming hot. Serve at once.

To microwave: Place the mushrooms on a round micro-safe platter covered with a double layer of paper toweling; cover loosely with wax paper. Microwave on high for 2 minutes or until hot.

Yield: 12 appetizer servings. *Each stuffed mushroom provides: 49 cal, 5 g pro, 1.2 g unsat fat, 20 mg sodium, 10 mg chol.*

Tuna with Marinated Artichoke Hearts

The artichokes provide the marinade that brings an explosion of flavors to this piquant dish.

1 *jar (6 ounces) marinated artichoke hearts*
½ *cup whole pitted olives*
1½ *cups sliced mushrooms*
⅓ *cup olive oil*
2 *tablespoons red wine or balsamic vinegar*
2 *tablespoons lemon juice*
1 *large clove of garlic, minced*

⅛ *teaspoon freshly ground pepper*
½ *teaspoon dill weed*
1 *can (6½ ounces) chunk light tuna, water-packed and drained*
½ *teaspoon dill weed*
crisp romaine leaves
½ *cup sliced almonds, lightly toasted*

Drain and reserve the artichoke marinade. Arrange artichokes, olives, and mushrooms in a 3-quart shallow baking dish. In a screw-top jar, combine the reserved marinade, oil, vinegar, lemon juice, garlic, pepper, and dill. Cover the jar and shake it well. Pour it over the vegetables. Cover the dish and refrigerate for at least one hour.

Drain the marinade into a cruet or small pitcher. Fold the tuna into the marinated vegetables. Spoon onto small plates lined with romaine. Pour additional marinade dressing over each serving. Garnish with toasted almonds.

Yield: 10 servings. *Each serving provides: 115 cal, 5.2 g pro, 2.2 g sat fat, 4 g unsat fat, 8.4 mg chol.*

Herring Salad with Potatoes, Beets, and Apples

Just recalling this dish makes my mouth water. It's that sensational and so easy to put together.

1 cup pickled herring	1 large Granny Smith apple,
2 beets, boiled, or 1 can of	cored but not peeled
sliced beets	3 slices medium-size red onion
4 medium-size potatoes,	¼ cup vinaigrette dressing
boiled and cooled	2 tablespoons chopped
	walnuts

Discard the onion slices that come with the herring and drain. Cut the herring, beets, potatoes, and apple into half-inch cubes. Dice the onion. Combine all ingredients in a bowl. Add vinaigrette to taste and sprinkle with walnuts.

Yield: 10 servings. *Each serving provides: 114 cal, 5.1 g pro, .4 g sat fat, .4 g unsat fat.*

Sardine and Cottage Cheese Spread

Sardines are little, but oh boy, they pack a nutritional wallop that's hard to beat. For a lovely marriage of distinctive flavors, enjoy this spread on toast points or toasted pita, or stuff it into celery.

2 cans (3¼ ounces each)
    sardines
½ cup low-fat ricotta or
    drained cottage cheese
2 shallots, scallions, or ½
    small onion; finely
    minced

1 tablespoon chopped parsley
½ teaspoon paprika
    pinch of cayenne pepper
2 tablespoons lemon juice

Drain sardines well. In a flat bowl, mash the sardines. Combine with the remaining ingredients and mix to blend. Makes ¾ cup.

Yield: 8 servings. *Each serving provides: 36.3 cal, 4 g pro, .8 g fat.*

Darling Little Cheese Balls

1 can (3¼ ounces) sardines
4 ounces reduced-calorie
    cream cheese
1 teaspoon Worcestershire
    sauce

2 gratings of pepper or to
    taste
½ cup finely chopped nuts
    (any kind)

Drain sardines well. In a bowl, mash them with a fork. Add the cheese, Worcestershire sauce, and pepper. Mix until well blended and smooth. Cover bowl and refrigerate until chilled. Form into small balls of about ¾-inch-diameter. Roll in chopped nuts. Place cocktail pick in each ball. Chill and serve.

Yield: 15 balls. *Each cheese ball provides: 40 cal, .66 g pro, 1 g sat fat, 1 g unsat fat.*

Curried Tuna Pinwheels

This easy-to-prepare hors d'oeuvre is a taste sensation. It can be prepared ahead, up to the broiling. Broil just before serving.

1 can chunk-style tuna, packed in water and drained
½ teaspoon curry powder
1 tablespoon grated onion
6 tablespoons plain yogurt
2 tablespoons reduced-calorie mayonnaise
14 slices fresh whole-grain or enriched white bread
paprika

In a medium-size bowl or food processor, blend together the tuna, curry powder, grated onion, yogurt, and mayonnaise until creamy. Trim crusts from the bread. (Reserve them and toast them lightly for bread sticks.) Spread each slice of bread with the tuna mixture. Sprinkle with paprika.

Roll up each slice jelly-roll fashion. Wrap securely in waxed paper and chill for 6 hours or overnight. Before serving, slice each roll crosswise into 3 pieces.

(continued)

Place on cookie sheet lined with parchment paper or sprayed with cooking spray. Broil until golden, about 3 minutes; turn and toast the other side. Serve hot.

Yield: 42 pinwheels. *Each pinwheel provides: 24.7 cal, 2 g pro, .5 g fat.*

Chopped Herring with Applesance

This is an easy way to make the lovely chopped herring so popular in Jewish cuisine.

1 cup pickled herring
¼ cup chopped red onion

½ cup unsweetened applesauce

Drain the herring and remove onions. In a food processor, blend together the herring, red onion, and applesauce. Add additional applesauce if needed, to make a light, chunky texture.

Yield: 2 cups. *Each tablespoon provides: 39.7 cal, 2.4 g pro, .28 g sat fat, .28 g unsat fat.*

Pickled Salmon

2½ cups water
1 cup white vinegar
4 onions, sliced
2 teaspoons herbal seasoning
2 tablespoons honey

1 tablespoon pickling spices
2 pounds fresh salmon steaks,
   cut in 1-inch chunks

In a medium-size saucepan, combine water, vinegar, and half of the sliced onions. Bring to a boil and continue on a slow boil for 15 minutes. Add the herbal seasoning, honey, pickling spices, and salmon chunks. Simmer for 10 minutes or until salmon flakes easily with a fork. With a slotted spoon, remove the fish to a deep bowl.

Layer the remaining onion slices between the chunks of salmon. Pour the cooking liquid, unstrained, over the fish and cover tightly.

Yield: 8 to 10 servings. *Each of 10 servings provides: 150 cal, 22 g pro, 3.8 g unsat fat, 52 mg sodium, 74 mg chol.*

Salmon Torta Appetizer

This dish works just as well with tuna. It is excellent served either hot or at room temperature—wonderfully welcome at bring-a-dish parties.

1 can (7½ ounces) pink
   salmon
4 eggs
1½ cups unpeeled shredded
   zucchini
¼ cup oat bran
¼ cup wheat germ

¼ cup whole-wheat pastry
   flour
2 tablespoons lecithin
   granules (optional)
½ cup plain yogurt
½ cup diced onion
1 teaspoon tarragon
2 tablespoons sesame seeds

Drain the salmon and reserve.

In the bowl of food processor, combine the eggs, zucchini, oat bran, wheat germ, flour, lecithin granules, yogurt, onion, and tarragon. Process to combine ingredients. Add the salmon and mix well. Pour the mixture into a 1½-quart shallow glass baking dish. Drizzle sesame seeds on top. Bake in a 350-degree oven for 35 minutes or until firm and golden. Cut into one-inch-square pieces.

Yield: 35 pieces. *Each piece provides: 22 cal, 2.6 g pro, .3 g sat fat, .5g unsat fat, 30 mg sodium, 34 mg chol.*

Shad Roe Appetizer

This zippy appetizer tastes sinfully good but, in fact, is very low in calories and fat.

1 shad roe	¼ teaspoon freshly ground
1 cup dry white wine	pepper
1 teaspoon herbal seasoning	2 tablespoons mustard
	1 tablespoon horseradish

In a saucepan combine the roe, wine, herbal seasonings, and pepper. Heat to the boiling point, then simmer for about 20 minutes or until the roe is cooked through. Drain and chill for several hours in the refrigerator. In a small glass bowl, combine the mustard and horse-radish.

Slice the roe thin and serve on crackers spread with the horse-radish sauce.

Yield: about 10 slices. *Each slice provides: about 10 cal, 1.5 g pro, .3 unsat fat, 3.6 mg sodium.*

18

SALADS

Fish salads can be made in infinite variety, and they give you a wonderful opportunity to combine complementary nutrients, textures, and flavors. Salads bring fiber, color, and crunch to the protein and the Omega-3 fatty acids that you get in fish.

Any cooked fish can be a wholesome ingredient in a salad. In the following recipes I have put the emphasis on tuna and salmon because they turned out to be the best fish for lowering LDL, or "bad" cholesterol, and because these fish are generally available in cans.

Several different kinds of fish are sold as tuna. The lightest of these, albacore, is labeled "white meat." All the others are labeled "light meat."

The three different forms in which tuna is packed refer to the size of the pieces in the can: chunk-style, flaked, and grated. All represent good-quality tuna. Always check the label when you buy tuna to see if it's packed in water or oil. Water-packed tuna has less oil and fewer calories than the oil-packed, even when the oil-packed is well drained.

To reduce the salt content of canned tuna, dump it into a strainer and give it a cold-water shower.

188

Tuna and Pasta Salad with Pine Nuts and Red Peppers

If pine nuts are unavailable, use sunflower seeds or chopped almonds.

1   tablespoon olive or canola oil
½   cup pine nuts
2   cloves garlic, minced
1   large tomato, peeled and
    coarsely chopped
One 6½- to 7-ounce can
    water-packed tuna,
    drained
One 5-ounce jar roasted red
    peppers or pimentos, cut
    in strips

½   cup pitted black olives,
    coarsely chopped
2   tablespoons balsamic or
    red-wine vinegar
    freshly ground pepper, to
    taste
1   pound regular or spinach
    fettuccine or linguine
2   tablespoons minced parsley

In a heavy skillet, heat the oil. Add the pine nuts and cook until lightly browned, about 2 minutes. Stir in the garlic and cook until golden, about 1 minute more. Stir in the tomato. Transfer the mixture to a large bowl. Stir in the tuna, red peppers, olives, vinegar, and pepper. At this point, the tuna sauce can be covered and allowed to stand at room temperature for up to 2 hours.

Meanwhile, cook the pasta according to package directions until it is *al dente*. Drain in colander, then add the pasta to the tuna sauce and mix well. Sprinkle with the parsley. Serve at room temperature.

Yield: 6 servings. *Each salad provides: 216 cal, 11.4 g pro, .2 g sat fat, 2 g unsat fat.*

Salmon Salad with Yogurt and Cucumber

In this recipe, yogurt provides all the moisture needed and a touch of cool tartness that accents and enhances the flavor of the salmon. Serve on crisp salad greens or in pockets of lightly toasted whole-wheat pita.

1 cup cooked or canned
    salmon, flaked
1 small cucumber, diced
6 tablespoons plain yogurt
2 teaspoons lemon juice

1 tablespoon chopped
    scallions or chives
salad greens
whole-wheat pita, halved

In a glass bowl, combine all the ingredients except the salad greens and pita. Chill.

Yield: 3 servings. *Each serving provides: 166 cal, 12.4 g pro, 2 g sat fat, 4 g unsat fat.*

Tuna and Potato Salad Niçoise

This Mediterranean salad with its built-in salad dressing is a most satisfying one-dish meal. Enjoy it with a hunk of crusty Italian bread or a toasted whole-wheat pita.

2 tablespoons dry white wine
2 tablespoons wine or balsamic vinegar
½ teaspoon pepper, or to taste
⅓ cup olive oil
2 tablespoons minced green onions or chives
1 tablespoon minced parsley
½ teaspoon crushed oregano

8 medium-size potatoes, cooked, then peeled and sliced
Boston lettuce or romaine leaves, or a combination of salad greens
1 cup green beans, cooked crisp but tender
1 can (6½ ounces) water-packed tuna, drained
3 hard-cooked eggs, quartered

In a large bowl, combine wine, vinegar, and pepper. Stir in the oil. Remove and reserve ¼ cup of this dressing.

To the remaining dressing in the bowl, stir in the onions, oregano, and parsley. Add the potatoes and toss gently until each slice is coated with dressing. Cover and refrigerate 2 hours to allow flavors to meld. To serve, line a platter with lettuce leaves; arrange potato salad, beans, tuna, and eggs on the lettuce. Pour reserved dressing over all.

Yield: 4 servings. *Each serving provides: 416 cal, 30 g pro, 3 g sat fat, 22 g unsat fat.*

Tuna Ambrosia Salad
with Pineapple and Raisins

A delightful explosion of flavors, this salad is wonderful for a bridge or mah-jongg luncheon or a romantic patio repast. It provides a whole alphabet of wholesome nutrients to put energy in your body and a twinkle in your eye.

½ cup low-fat plain yogurt
2 tablespoons unsweetened flaked coconut
¼ cup raisins
1 teaspoon curry powder
1 can water-packed chunk light tuna, drained

1 can (8 ounces) crushed pineapple, drained
1 cup alfalfa sprouts
1 can mandarin oranges, drained
¼ cup toasted pine nuts, chopped almonds, or sunflower seeds

In a bowl, mix together the yogurt, coconut, raisins, and curry powder. Fold in the tuna and pineapple. Line four salad plates with alfalfa sprouts. Arrange orange sections around the outer edge of the sprouts. Spoon the tuna mixture into the center. Sprinkle each salad with pine nuts, almonds, or sunflower seeds.

Yield: 4 servings. *Each serving provides: 190 cal, 17.2 g pro, 1.6 g sat fat, 2.1 g unsat fat.*

Polynesian Tuna Salad

2 tablespoons mayonnaise
2 tablespoons yogurt
1 tablespoon lemon juice
1 can (6½ ounces) tuna fish,
    drained
2 tablespoons raisins or
    currants

2 tablespoons chopped celery
4 slices canned pineapple,
    drained
½ cup chopped, toasted
    almonds
    sweet red pepper to garnish

In a mixing bowl, combine mayonnaise, yogurt, and lemon juice. Add tuna, raisins, or currants, and then celery. Mix to combine ingredients and refrigerate. To serve, place pineapple slices on top of chopped almonds; top with tuna mixture and sweet red pepper.

Yield: 2 to 4 servings. *Each serving provides: 215 cal, 18 g pro, 4.3 g sat fat, 11 g unsat fat, 82 mg sodium, 42 mg chol.*

Hot and Cold Grilled Salmon Salad

I enjoyed this salad at Parks' Seafood Restaurant in my hometown, Allentown, Pennsylvania. Fred Parks, the chef, graciously shared the recipe with me and I am happy to share it with you.

4 salmon fillets (4 to 5 ounces each)

½ cup teriyaki sauce

4 cups salad greens (using a mixture of romaine, parsley, and spinach)

4 pineapple slices (fresh or canned)

2 red onions, thinly sliced

3 tablespoons pineapple juice

4 scallions, coarsely chopped

Place the salmon in a shallow bowl and brush each piece with the teriyaki sauce. Cover the dish and allow the fish to marinate for at least one hour. Prepare the salad greens and refrigerate.

Cut each pineapple slice into four chunks. Alternate the pineapple chunks and the onion slices in a circle around the greens.

Grill the salmon and broil it about 6 minutes on one side. Brush it with the reserved marinade; turn and broil 4 minutes on the flip side.

To prepare the dressing, bring the reserved marinade to a boil, then simmer for a few minutes. Combine 3 tablespoons of the marinade with the pineapple juice and whisk together.

Place the hot salmon on the chilled greens. Sprinkle with the scallions and drizzle with the dressing.

Yield: 4 servings. *Each serving provides: 295 cal, 5.34 g pro, 5 g sat fat, 5.4 g unsat fat, 85 mg sodium, 66 mg chol.*

19

GUMBOS, CHOWDERS, AND OTHER CHOICE MEDLEYS

In this chapter you will discover the many tantalizing ways in which fish can bring you new culinary pleasures and nutritional advantages.

While fish is a complete protein food, providing all the essential amino acids plus a whole roster of vitamins and minerals, it does lack fiber. When you combine fish with vegetables and grains—in the form of gumbos, stews, or chowders—you must provide the missing element. Doing so, you will also make a little go a long long way. And when prices are sky-high, that is no small consideration.

Fish Gumbo with Bananas

You may never have thought of combining fish and bananas, but you will find that the bananas add a pleasant, sweet counterpoint to the tartness of the tomatoes.

2 tablespoons butter or oil
½ cup chopped onion
¼ cup finely chopped green pepper
1 clove garlic, minced
1 tablespoon flour
2 cups chicken or vegetable broth
2 cups chopped tomatoes
⅓ cup chopped parsley
1 small bay leaf

¼ teaspoon thyme
⅛ teaspoon freshly ground pepper
2 pounds fish fillets, cut into 2-inch chunks
1 teaspoon lemon juice
1 teaspoon reduced-sodium soy sauce
⅛ teaspoon cayenne pepper
4 bananas, cut into 1-inch chunks

In a large, heavy pot, heat the butter or oil. Add onion, green pepper, and garlic. Cook about 5 minutes or until soft. Add flour and cook for 2 minutes, stirring constantly. While stirring, pour in the broth. Add the tomatoes, parsley, bay leaf, thyme, and pepper. Bring to a boil, reduce the heat, and simmer, partially covered, for 20 minutes. Add fish and simmer for another 10 minutes. Discard the bay leaf. Stir in lemon juice, soy sauce, cayenne, and bananas. Serve with hot cooked brown rice.

To microwave: If you're a calorie counter, eliminate the fat. Fish will remain moist. In a 4-quart micro-safe casserole, micro-cook the onion, pepper, and garlic with one tablespoon broth or water for about 2 minutes on high and uncovered. Stir in the flour. Add only 1½ cups broth, the tomatoes, parsley, bay leaf, thyme, and pepper. Micro-cook for 8 minutes. Add the fish. Microwave, covered with vented plastic wrap, on high for 4 minutes. Proceed as in conventional recipe above.

If you prepare this dish without the fat, the calorie count drops to 360, the fat drops to zero, and the sodium to 383 mg.

Yield: 6 servings. *Each serving provides: 400 cal, 32 g pro, 1 g sat fat, .5 g unsat fat, 483 mg sodium, 60 mg chol.*

Salmon Spaghetti

This sounds far out, doesn't it? Well, don't knock it. It is tasty, immensely satisfying, and so easy to prepare—even on the spur of the moment.

1½ cups sliced mushrooms
¼ cup sliced green onions
2 tablespoons butter or olive oil
1 can (15½ ounces) pink salmon with liquid
3 tablespoons dry white wine
1 pound whole-wheat or spinach spaghetti, cooked
1 cup plain yogurt
1 tablespoon whole-wheat flour
⅛ teaspoon freshly ground pepper

Sauté mushrooms and onions in butter or oil over low heat until vegetables are just tender. Add salmon, with its liquid, and the wine. Simmer for 3 minutes. Combine yogurt, flour, and pepper. Stir into

(continued)

the salmon mixture in the skillet. Cook, stirring, for 3 minutes longer. Serve over the hot cooked spaghetti.

Yield: 4 servings. *Each serving provides: 401 cal, 33 g pro, 1.6 g sat fat, .9 g unsat fat, 521 mg sodium, 62 mg chol.*

Hearty Fish Stew

When you have a whole fish filleted at the market, be sure to ask for the head and carcass. They're great for fish stock, soups, and stews, as used in the following recipe.

bones, head, and skin of any	2 *ribs celery, diced*
fish, preferably salmon	2 *potatoes*
6 *cups water*	1½ *cups flaked cooked fish*
1 *onion, chopped*	*minced parsley for garnish*
2 *tablespoons butter*	

Place fish bones, head, and skin in a soup kettle with the water. Allow to simmer for 30 minutes. Strain and discard fish scraps. Sauté onion in butter until limp. Add celery and cook briefly. Dice potatoes, add to broth, and simmer until tender.

Add flaked fish. Simmer a few more minutes to heat the fish. Serve hot, garnished with parsley.

Yield: 6 to 8 servings. *Each of 6 servings provides: 133 cal, 6.5 g pro, 1.6 g sat fat, .9 g unsat fat, 66 mg sodium, 20 mg chol.*

Elegant Tuna Bisque
with Flaky Puff-Pastry Top Hat

This easy-to-prepare, inexpensive dish looks like a million bucks and tastes heavenly.

1 package (10 ounces) frozen creamed spinach, thawed	¼ teaspoon pepper
1 cup vegetable broth or water	1 can (7 ounces) tuna fish, water-packed, drained
2 cups milk	6 frozen patty shells (10-ounce package), defrosted
½ cup grated Parmesan cheese	
2 tablespoons chopped chives	
1 teaspoon dried basil	1 egg, lightly beaten

In mixing bowl or food processor, combine spinach and broth; process until smooth. Add milk, cheese, chives, basil, and pepper. Divide tuna equally among six oven-proof, 1½-cup soup bowls. Pour soup mixture into bowls.

With a rolling pin, roll each patty shell into a 6-inch circle. Lay pastry on top of each bowl, leaving about a 1-inch overhang. Press the overhang firmly to the sides of the bowl.

Place the oven rack in the lower third of the oven and preheat to 400 degrees. Brush each pastry with the beaten egg.

Bake for 10 to 15 minutes or until pastry is puffed and golden brown. To eat, break up the pastry dome with a spoon and stir it into the soup. It will become thick and creamy.

Yield: 6 servings. *Each serving provides: 381 cal, 19 g pro, 5 g sat fat, 33 g unsat fat, 299 mg sodium, 25 mg chol.*

Fish and Vegetable Chowder

This zesty, bone-warming bowl of cheer puts a glow on your face.

1½ pounds of fresh or frozen
    fish fillets (haddock or
    other lean white fish)
2 tablespoons butter or olive
    oil
¼ cup chopped celery
¼ cup chopped onion
¼ cup whole-wheat flour
1 teaspoon herbal seasoning
½ teaspoon dried marjoram,
    crushed

3 cups reconstituted nonfat
    dry milk or low-fat milk
1 package (10 ounces) frozen
    mixed vegetables or one
    16-ounce can mixed
    vegetables, drained
1 cup shredded reduced-fat,
    reduced-sodium
    mozzarella cheese
    (optional)

If fish is frozen, allow it to thaw.

Cut fillets into ¾-inch pieces. In a saucepan, heat the butter or oil. Add chopped celery and onion and cook till tender but not brown. Blend in the flour and seasonings. Add milk and water all at once. Cook and stir until thickened and bubbly.

Stir in the mixed vegetables. Cover and simmer for 10 minutes. Add fish pieces and shredded cheese, if you're using it. Cook about 5 minutes or till fish flakes easily and the cheese is melted.

Yield: 6 servings. *Each serving without cheese provides: 215 cal, 24 g pro, 2.1 g sat fat, 1.1 g unsat fat, 202 mg sodium, 41 mg chol.*

Each serving with cheese provides: 284 cal, 28.3 g pro, 5.2 g sat fat, 3 g unsat fat, 352 mg sodium, 65 mg chol.

Tuna Cashew Casserole

Here is an old favorite that excites a nostalgic glow. It is always a favorite at jolly bring-a-dish buffets, where it never fails to get raves and requests for the recipe. Guests are always amazed to hear it's made from tuna. It tastes much more exotic.

1 can (10½ ounces) cream of
    mushroom soup,
    undiluted
¼ cup water
1 can water-packed tuna,
    drained
¼ cup minced onion
1 cup diced celery

dash of pepper
1 can (3½ ounces) chow mein
    noodles or 1 cup oat-bran
    crunch
½ cup cashew nuts
2 tablespoons oat bran
2 tablespoons wheat germ

Combine mushroom soup, water, tuna, onion, celery, and pepper in a 1½-quart casserole. Bake, uncovered, for 40 minutes in a 325-degree oven. Remove from oven and stir in the noodles or oat-bran crunch, cashew nuts, oat bran, and wheat germ.

To microwave: Combine all ingredients in a 2-quart casserole. Microwave on high for 5 minutes.

Yield: 6 servings. *Each serving provides: 216 cal, 8.4 g pro, 2.5 g sat fat, 8 g unsat fat, 410 mg sodium, 25 mg chol.*

Aunt Betty's Fish Stroganoff

This is a delightful dish. It makes leftover fish more exotic than its original presentation. Fried green tomatoes are a lovely accompaniment. (See page 292 for recipe.) If you don't have any leftover fish, try it with 2 cans of tuna or salmon.

2 tablespoons butter or olive
   oil
1 cup sliced mushrooms
¼ cup chopped green or red
   pepper
1 onion, chopped
2 cloves garlic, finely chopped
1 can (10½ ounces) condensed
   tomato soup
1 cup yogurt

½ cup milk
1 tablespoon Worcestershire
   sauce
¼ teaspoon red pepper sauce,
   or Tabasco®
herbal seasoning and
   pepper to taste
1½ to 2 cups cooked fish, flaked

In a large skillet or heavy saucepan, heat the butter or oil. Add the mushrooms, pepper, onion, and garlic and sauté until tender. In a bowl, combine the soup, yogurt, milk, Worcestershire, red pepper sauce (or Tabasco®), and herbal seasonings. Add this mixture slowly to the mushroom mixture, stirring constantly until the mixture reaches the boiling point. Add the flaked fish and serve over brown rice, noodles, or whole-grain toast.

Yield: 6 servings. *Each serving (without the noodles, rice, or toast) provides: 124 cal, 9.6 g pro, 2.5 g sat fat, 2 g unsat fat, 486 mg sodium, 30 mg chol.*

Red Snapper Soup

Here's a real energy booster. Whenever I feel droopy, especially when I was pregnant, I cherish a hot bowl of this fragrant soup. I serve it for lunch on the day I make it, then freeze the remaining soup in one-bowl portions. Stop in for lunch. I'll have it hot out of the microwave for you in three minutes.

1 red snapper (about 1 pound)
2½ cups vegetable stock or water
1 tablespoon pickling spices
1 teaspoon herbal seasoning
1 tablespoon unsalted butter or oil

¼ cup chopped onion
½ cup chopped celery
½ cup diced green pepper
1 cup broth or water
1 can tomato soup
½ cup sherry

Place fish in a skillet. Add 2½ cups water or stock, pickling spices, and herbal seasoning. Cover and simmer for 10 to 15 minutes. Strain the broth and reserve. Remove fish from skillet and reserve.

Heat the butter or oil in the skillet. Add the onion, celery, and green pepper and lightly sauté. Add the reserved fish stock and simmer gently. Stir in the broth and tomato soup. Bone and skin the fish and add it to the soup. Stir in the sherry.

Yield: about 2 quarts or 8 servings. *Each serving provides: 123 cal, 19.5 g pro, 1.5 g sat fat, 2.9 g unsat fat, 148 mg sodium, 40 mg chol.*

Brown and Crispy Salmon Cakes

These can be made with canned salmon or with leftover cooked salmon or other leftover fish. As a change from the yogurt dill sauce, try it, the second time around, with hot spaghetti sauce.

1 can (14¾ ounces) salmon, drained
1 tablespoon unsalted butter
½ cup chopped onion
½ cup chopped celery
1 egg, lightly beaten
¼ cup reduced-calorie mayonnaise
juice of half a lemon
3 tablespoons chopped fresh dill

2 teaspoons dry mustard
1 teaspoon herbal seasoning
½ teaspoon freshly ground pepper
¼ cup fresh bread crumbs
2 tablespoons whole-wheat pastry flour
1 tablespoon canola or olive oil
3 tablespoons chopped fresh dill
1 cup yogurt

Place the salmon in a mixing bowl and flake it into bite-size pieces. Break up the skin and bones and include them with the salmon.

Heat the butter and sauté the onion and celery until softened. Set aside.

In a small bowl, stir together the egg, mayonnaise, lemon juice, chopped dill, mustard, herbal seasoning, and pepper. Add this mixture, along with the bread crumbs and the onion-celery mixture, to the salmon. The mixture should be moist. Cover the mixture and refrigerate for about an hour.

On a sheet of waxed paper, spread the flour. Heat the oil in a wide, non-stick skillet. Form the fish mixture into fish cakes and carefully flour both sides of each one. Sauté the cakes over moderate heat, until they are golden, about 4 minutes. With a spatula, turn and cook the flip sides until golden, about 3 minutes. Serve with dilled yogurt (3 tablespoons chopped dill combined with 1 cup of yogurt).

Yield: 6 to 8 servings. *Each serving (of 6) provides: 17 cal, 26 g pro, 4 g sat fat, 9 g unsat fat, 426 mg sodium, 62 mg chol.*

Salmon Cucumber Soup

1 can (7¾ ounces) salmon
4 small cucumbers
1 medium-size onion, chopped
1 cup vegetable, fish, or chicken broth
2 tablespoons lemon juice

½ teaspoon freshly grated pepper
1 teaspoon fresh dill, chopped, or ½ teaspoon dried dill
1 cup yogurt
toasted sesame seeds
paprika

Flake the salmon. Peel the cucumbers if they have been waxed, and cut them in chunks. Place salmon with its liquid, cucumbers, and onion in food processor or blender. Process until smooth. Add broth, lemon juice, pepper, and dill. Puree thoroughly. Stir in the yogurt. Chill.

Serve in chilled bowls. Garnish with toasted sesame seeds and paprika.

Yield: 4 to 6 servings. *Each serving (of 4) provides: 100 cal, 9 g pro, 1.1 g sat fat, .5 g unsat fat, 8 mg sodium, 0 mg chol.*

20

THE LEAN FAMILY:

Tilapia, Sole, Flounder, Haddock, Halibut, Scrod, Orange Roughy, Red Snapper, Cod, Perch, Bass, Tile, Pollack, Grouper

All fish are not created equal. Some are fat (over 6 percent fat content), providing about 150 calories in 3½ ounces. Some are moderately fat (2 to 6 percent fat), with about 114 calories in 3½ ounces. And some are lean (under 2 percent fat), providing about 82 calories in 3½ ounces. The lean family outnumbers its fattier cousins, and includes: black sea bass, cod, croaker, flounder, fluke, gray sole, grouper, haddock, halibut, lemon sole, lingcod, perch, pollack, red snapper, rockfish, scrod, skate, and tilefish. Lean fish can be prepared by any method of cooking. However, when broiling or baking it, the lean fish usually needs a little more butter, oil, or other moistener to prevent its drying out.

CREATIVE LEFTOVERS

I like to prepare more fish than I need for dinner because the leftover cooked fish is so tasty and so versatile. Try serving it with a cocktail sauce made from equal amounts of ketchup and horseradish and it tastes like a shrimp cocktail. Serve it with hot, melted butter as a dipping sauce and it tastes like lobster. In fact, this dish is called Poor Man's Lobster. A more elegant version, described below, is called Mock Lobster à la Newburgh.

The fish specified in the following recipes are the ones I used in testing the recipes. However, any member of the lean family may be substituted for the one indicated.

Simply Broiled Haddock

Haddock is the most popular fish in the market, says Paul Heckenberger, who presides over a very lively fish market in my hometown, Allentown, Pennsylvania. Haddock is Paul's favorite, too, and this is his favorite way to prepare it.

1 pound of haddock fillets	*½ cup seasoned whole-wheat*
1 tablespoon melted butter	*flour or bread crumbs*
1 tablespoon lemon juice	*1 teaspoon paprika*

Brush the fillets with a mixture of the butter and lemon juice. Dust with the flour or bread crumbs mixed with the paprika. Place in a baking dish greased with butter or oil or sprayed with nonfat cooking spray. Place in oven heated to 400 degrees, about 4 inches from the heat for 8 to 12 minutes, or until opaque throughout.

Yield: 4 servings. *Each serving provides: 180 cal, 22 g pro, 1 g sat fat, 1.5 g unsat fat, 60 mg sodium, 65 mg chol.*

Broiled Haddock Fillets with Fresh Grapefruit

This is a feast for the eyes, the taste buds, and the body—providing protein, vitamins, and minerals in the fish, high bioflavonoid and vitamin C in the grapefruit, and fiber in the bread cubes.

1½ pounds haddock fillets
1 teaspoon herbal seasoning
⅛ teaspoon freshly ground
   pepper
¾ cup small bread cubes
   (preferably whole grain)

2 tablespoons olive or canola
   oil or melted butter
½ teaspoon dried thyme
12 fresh grapefruit sections

Wipe the fillets with a damp cloth. Sprinkle both sides with the herbal seasoner and pepper. Place in a shallow buttered or oiled baking pan.

Mix the bread cubes with 1 tablespoon of the butter or oil and the thyme. Sprinkle the cubes over the fish. Top with grapefruit sections. Brush with the remaining butter or oil. Place under broiler with oven set to 400 degrees. Broil for 10 minutes or until fish is flaky and crumbs are brown.

Yield: 6 servings. *Each serving provides: 143 cal, 24.4 g pro, 1.4 g sat fat, 3.4 g unsat fat, 62 mg sodium, 65 mg chol.*

Baked Stuffed Haddock Fillets

Here is a very special high-fiber presentation to glamorize any member of the lean-fish family.

2 fillets of haddock (about 1½ pounds)
2 tablespoons lemon juice
½ cup fresh bread crumbs
2 tablespoons wheat germ
2 tablespoons oat bran
2 tablespoons melted butter
⅔ cup low-fat milk
1 cup sliced mushrooms
½ teaspoon herbal seasoning
¼ teaspoon freshly ground pepper

Place one fillet in a baking dish greased with butter, oil, or cooking spray.

Combine bread crumbs, wheat germ, oat bran, and melted butter. Reserve half of the bread-crumb mixture. Add the chopped mushrooms, mixed with the herbal seasoning and pepper, to the remaining crumb mixture. Place this mushroom mixture on the fillet in the baking dish. Cover with the other fillet. Pour milk over the top.

Preheat oven to 450 degrees. Brown the fish for about 5 minutes. Reduce heat to 350 degrees and bake for 25 minutes, basting with pan juices. Sprinkle with reserved crumbs and bake until crumbs are brown. Sprinkle with lemon juice.

Yield: 6 servings. *Each serving provides: 171.5 cal, 20.7 g pro, 3 g sat fat, 2 g unsat fat, 176 mg sodium, 65 mg chol.*

Mock Lobster à la Newburgh

This is a very special dish. Reserve it for great occasions.

2 pounds haddock fillets
2 tablespoons butter
2 tablespoons flour
3 egg yolks, beaten
½ cup low-fat milk

½ cup whole milk or light
    cream
3 tablespoons dry white wine
2 teaspoons lemon juice
1 teaspoon herbal seasoning
1 teaspoon paprika

Poach the fish in very little water or steam it in a steamer, strainer, or colander over boiling water. Don't let the water touch the fish. Steam for 10 minutes. Let the fish cool, then flake it.

In the top part of a double-boiler, melt the butter. Blend in the flour. Combine the milks and add all at once. Cook and stir until thick and bubbly. Place over hot water in the bottom part of the double-boiler. Stir a few tablespoons of the mixture into the beaten egg yolks. Return to the hot mixture. Cook, stirring constantly, until thickened. Add the flaked fish and heat through. Stir in the wine, lemon juice, and herbal seasoning. Sprinkle with paprika. Serve over cooked brown rice, in patty shells or on toast.

Yield: 6 to 8 servings. *Each serving (of 8) of the fish mixture provides: 142 cal, 20.6 g pro, 2 g sat fat, 1.15 g unsat fat, 80 mg sodium, 178 mg chol.*

Louisiana Halibut

A flat fish, halibut is firm, lean, and white—thicker and more moist than the other flat fish. It is sweet and delicious whether it is grilled, baked, or poached and combines well with many different sauces. It is available as fillets or steaks. In this Louisiana version, a halibut steak is baked with onions and green peppers, which add important fiber and vitamin C. The tomato soup provides lots of vitamin A, which is a boon to your eyes, your complexion, and your ability to resist infections. This is a very wholesome and tasty dish and very easy to prepare.

1 pound halibut steak
1 teaspoon herbal seasoning
1 large green pepper, chopped
1 large onion, chopped
1 can (10 ounces) tomato soup
¼ teaspoon freshly ground
    pepper, or to taste

Place the halibut steak in a baking dish that has been greased with butter, oil, or cooking spray. Sprinkle with the herbal seasoning and the freshly ground pepper. Combine the green peppers, onions, and tomato soup. Pour this mixture over the fish. Bake in a 350-degree conventional oven for 20 to 25 minutes, or until it is opaque clear through; or in your microwave oven on high for 5 to 8 minutes.

Yield: 4 servings. *Each serving provides: 178 cal, 22.5 g pro, 0 g sat fat, 1.6 g unsat fat, 655 mg sodium, 49 mg chol.*

Note: If you wish to use this method of preparation for fillet of halibut or any member of the lean flatfish family, reduce the baking time in the conventional oven to 20 minutes, then check for doneness. If you're using the microwave oven, reduce the time to 5 minutes, then check.

Peasant-Style Fish Steaks in Garlic and Wine

The onions and garlic in this flavorful dish provide a goodly amount of allicin, a substance that has been shown to inhibit the formation of blood clots.

4 *large cloves fresh garlic, minced*
1 *tablespoon lemon juice*
2 *pounds halibut or other white-fish steaks*
1 *teaspoon herbal seasoning*
½ *teaspoon paprika*
¼ *teaspoon white pepper, or to taste*

1 *tablespoon olive or canola oil*
½ *tablespoon butter*
6 *thin tomato slices*
6 *thin onion slices*
6 *thin green pepper slices*
¼ *cup white wine vinegar*
2 *tablespoons water*
¼ *teaspoon dried dill parsley*

Combine 1 clove of minced garlic with lemon juice. Set aside. Combine herbal seasoning, paprika, and pepper. Sprinkle this mixture over the fish steaks.

In a skillet, brown one side of the fish steaks in the heated oil and butter. Turn the fish over and discard any excess fat in the pan. Spread the top of each steak with the garlic mixture. Top with tomato, onion, and pepper slices. Cover the skillet and cook until fish flakes easily with a fork—about 10 to 15 minutes, depending on the thickness of the steaks.

Remove the fish and vegetables to a heated serving platter. To the skillet, add the vinegar, water, dill, and remaining 3 cloves of minced garlic. Bring to a boil, reduce heat, and simmer 2 or 3 minutes. Pour this sauce over the fish. Garnish with parsley. Serve hot or cold. It's excellent either way.

Yield: 6 servings. *Each serving provides: 245 cal, 45 g pro, 3 g sat fat, 12 g unsat fat, 207 mg sodium, 52 mg chol.*

Fillet of Sole Poached
in Pineapple and Grape Juice

Whether you use flounder, Dover sole, or any light-fleshed lean fish, this is an elegantly delicious presentation, rich in fiber, vitamin C, and important minerals and enzymes. Orange or apricot juice may be substituted for the grape juice.

1 *cup white grape juice*
½ *cup unsweetened pineapple*
    juice
2 *teaspoons lemon juice*
½ *teaspoon ground ginger*

2 *pounds fillet of sole*
1 *cup unsweetened pineapple*
    chunks
½ *cup sliced almonds, lightly*
    toasted

In a large skillet, bring to a boil the grape juice, pineapple juice, lemon juice, and ginger. Add the fish, lower the heat, and poach the fish until it flakes—about 7 minutes.

To avoid breaking the fish, use two spatulas to remove it from the poaching liquid. Garnish with pineapple chunks and toasted almonds.

Yield: 6 servings. *Each serving provides: 221.3 cal, 24.56 g pro, 1 g sat fat, 11 g unsat fat, 58 mg sodium, 59 mg chol.*

Exotic Fish Fillet Stir-Fry

Enjoy the essence of Hawaii in this lovely quick-and-easy dish that delights the taste buds with its satisfying blend of sweet and tart.

1   can (20 ounces) unsweetened pineapple chunks
2   pounds halibut, flounder, sole, haddock, or scrod
2   tablespoons butter
1   teaspoon minced garlic
2   teaspoons curry powder
1   teaspoon herbal seasoning
1   large cucumber, thinly sliced
½   cup chopped green onions
2   tablespoons lemon juice
2   teaspoons arrowroot or cornstarch
3   cups hot cooked brown rice
    flaked unsweetened coconut (optional)

Drain the pineapple and reserve ½ cup of the juice. Cut the fish in bite-size pieces. In a large skillet, melt the butter. Add the garlic and sauté for 1 minute. Stir in the curry powder and cook until frothy. Add the fish and the herbal seasoning. Cook over medium heat for 4 minutes. Add cucumber and onions. Cook 1 minute. Stir in pineapple, lemon juice, and the reserved pineapple juice.

Mix arrowroot or cornstarch with 2 teaspoons of water. Stir into the fish mixture and cook until thickened—2 to 3 minutes. Serve over rice and top with coconut, if desired.

Yield: 6 servings. *Each serving, including the rice, provides: 171 cal, 5.2 g pro, 2 g sat fat, 1.2 g unsat fat, 91 mg sodium, 22 mg chol.*

Sole Almondine

Tell them you're having sole almondine and the children will turn off the TV and bounce into the kitchen. No leftovers! If you don't have any children to gobble it up, the leftovers make a lovely cold salad for the next day's lunch.

1½ pounds sole fillets
½ cup whole-wheat pastry flour
1 teaspoon herbal seasoning
½ teaspoon freshly grated pepper
⅓ cup milk
2 tablespoons canola or olive oil
2 tablespoons butter
2 tablespoons lemon juice
2 tablespoons sliced almonds

Cut fillets in six serving portions. Pat dry on paper towels. On wax paper, combine flour, herbal seasoning, and pepper. Dip fish pieces first into the milk, then into the flour mixture. In a large skillet, heat oil and butter.

Cook the fillets 6 to 8 minutes or until golden brown, turning once during cooking. Remove the fish and keep it warm. Pour the fat out of the skillet. Add the almonds and the lemon juice. Cook for about 30 seconds, then pour this mixture over the fish.

Yield: 6 servings. *Each serving provides: 280 cal, 30 g pro, 5 g sat fat, 6 g unsat fat, 80 mg sodium, 80 mg chol.*

Curried Flounder with Sweet Potatoes, Bananas, and Coconut

Serve this most unusual presentation on your favorite person's birthday. The sweet potatoes are an excellent source of the antioxidant beta-carotene that has been shown to not only retard the development of malignancies but also to reduce the incidence of myocardial infarction, stroke, and other adverse cardiovascular events among men with coronary disease. Bananas are a wonderful source of the potassium so important to your heart muscle. Together with the wonderful nutrients provided by the fish, this dish implies a wish for good health and a long, sweet life.

2 cups orange juice
½ teaspoon ground cinnamon
¼ teaspoon ground ginger
1 teaspoon curry powder, or
    to taste
¼ cup raisins
4 medium-size sweet
    potatoes, scrubbed and
    cut into ½-inch slices
2 pounds flounder or haddock
    fillets

1 large banana, peeled, sliced,
    and dipped in acidulated
    water (To make acidulated
    water, mix 1 tablespoon
    lemon juice or white
    vinegar with 1 quart
    water.)
½ cup grated unsweetened
    coconut, or toasted
    sunflower seeds

In a large, heavy pot, heat the orange juice to a boil. Add cinnamon, ginger, curry powder, raisins, and potatoes. Reduce heat to simmer, cover, and cook until potatoes are barely fork-tender, about 15 minutes. Push potatoes aside and add the fish fillets. The fish should be covered by the juice. If not, add more juice. Cover and simmer until the fish flakes, about 8 to 10 minutes.

Remove fish and potatoes to a heated platter. Spoon some liquid over all. Garnish with banana and sprinkle with coconut or toasted sunflower seeds. Serve the remaining juice on the side.

Yield: 6 servings. *Each serving provides: 338 cal, 20.7 g pro, 4.48 g sat fat, .6 g unsat fat, 82.75 mg sodium, 65 mg chol.*

Egg-Battered Fillets with Walnuts

These are easy, quick, and delicious, and light as a cloud. I like to serve them with an eggplant and banana dish, providing a whole spectrum of complementary nutrients. This recipe makes a little fish go a long way.

1 pound fresh or defrosted frozen scrod fillets, or any fish in the lean family
2 eggs
½ teaspoon herbal seasoning
1 tablespoon arrowroot or cornstarch
1 tablespoon canola or olive oil

1 tablespoon unsalted butter
2 green onions including tops, sliced or chopped
½ cup coarsely chopped walnuts
2 teaspoons lemon juice or sherry
1½ tablespoons water
¼ teaspoon paprika

If the fillets are thick, slice them horizontally, ½ inch thick. Cut the fish into 1½-inch squares. In a small bowl, beat eggs with the herbal

(continued)

seasoning. Add starch and beat well, preferably with a wire whisk. Add the fish to the egg mixture, turning to coat fish thoroughly.

In a large skillet, heat the oil, then add the butter. With a slotted spoon, remove the fish from the egg mixture and sauté without stirring until delicately browned. With a spatula, turn the fish and cook for another minute.

While the fish is cooking, add onion, walnuts, sherry or lemon juice, water, and paprika to the leftover egg mixture. Pour this mixture over the fish, cover with the lid, turn heat to medium-low, and cook until egg is set and fish is tender.

Yield: 4 servings. *Each serving provides: 202 cal, 9.6 g pro, 3.2 g sat fat, 27 g unsat fat, 30 mg sodium, 16 mg chol.*

Braided Orange Roughy

From the appearance and mild flavor of the lean, low-calorie fillets you've been enjoying, you would hardly suspect that the parent fish that swims around in the coastal waters of New Zealand is frightening to look upon. It gets its name from its orange spiny coat and the bony ridges on its large head. The fish is flash-frozen as soon as it leaves the water and is still frozen when it reaches our shores and is displayed in the fish markets. Because orange roughy has so little fat, it tends to be dry, and is best when prepared with a moist companion like tomatoes or other vegetables, or with fruits that will contribute moisture. Any recipe for a lean white fish such as cod, scrod, flounder, bass, haddock, or grouper would be fine for roughy, and vice versa. (This unusual presentation gives the fillets more body and more moisture.)

1 tablespoon unsalted butter
1 large onion, chopped
1 green or red pepper, chopped
2 tomatoes chopped, or 1 cup canned tomatoes, drained
1 teaspoon herbal seasoning

½ teaspoon freshly ground pepper
3 orange roughy fillets (about 1½ pounds)
2 tablespoons lemon juice
1 teaspoon paprika

In a large skillet, heat the butter and lightly sauté the onion, red and green pepper, and tomatoes. Blend in the herbal seasoning and black pepper. On a sheet of wax paper, slice the fillets lengthwise in 3 pieces each. Braid. Place the braids in an oven-proof oblong casserole. Arrange the sautéed vegetables on top and around the fish. Sprinkle with lemon juice and dust with paprika.

Bake in a 350-degree oven for 6 to 8 minutes or until fish is no longer translucent and flakes easily with a fork.

Yield: 6 servings. *Each serving provides: 125 cal, 17 g pro, 1.07 g sat fat, .7 g unsat fat, 76 mg sodium, 44 mg chol.*

Boxford Sole in Cream Sauce
with Asparagus and Mushrooms

This tastes like pure indulgence! You can use any firm white fish, such as orange roughy, cod, scrod, haddock, halibut—whatever is available. Asparagus, frequently used as a diuretic and long considered an aphrodisiac, is a good source of potassium, zinc, and also rutin, which toughens the walls of the blood vessels, thus helping to prevent dangerous ruptures. Put POW! in your sex life and enjoy your dinner.

1 pound sole fillets or any
    firm white fish
½ cup dry white wine
½ teaspoon herbal seasoning
1 cup cooked asparagus, cut
    in segments and drained
½ cup cherry tomato halves
½ cup sliced mushrooms
2 tablespoons unsalted butter

2 tablespoons whole-wheat
    flour
½ teaspoon pepper, or to taste
1¼ cups low-fat milk
1 egg yolk, lightly beaten
¼ cup dry white wine
1 cup soft bread crumbs,
    preferably whole grain
¼ cup grated Parmesan cheese

Poach the fish in ½ cup wine in a skillet, covered for 2 to 3 minutes or until fish flakes easily when pierced with a fork. Drain the poached fish and arrange it in a single layer in an oven-proof casserole. Sprinkle with the herbal seasoning. Top with asparagus, tomatoes, and mushrooms.

In a saucepan, melt the butter, then blend in the flour. Gradually stir in the milk, and cook, stirring, until sauce is smooth and thick. Stir a small amount of this sauce into the egg yolk, then return the egg-mixture sauce to the pot. Cook and stir until the mixture comes just to the boil. Remove from heat and stir in ¼ cup wine. Pour sauce over the fillets. Top with bread crumbs combined with the cheese. Bake at 350 degrees about 15 minutes.

Yield: 4 servings. *Each serving provides: 295 cal, 37 g pro, 5 g sat fat, 5 g unsat fat, 116 mg sodium, 50 mg chol.*

Fish Stock

Keep a supply of this in your freezer. It will enhance the flavor of many dishes. It can be used to replace water or white wine where these fluids are called for.

3 pounds meaty fish bones, preferably with head and tail on, but gills removed (Ask your friendly fishmonger to save them for you.)
6 cups water
1 cup dry white wine
1 cup coarsely chopped onion

4 sprigs parsley
1 cup coarsely chopped celery
1 bay leaf
½ teaspoon dried thyme
6 peppercorns
herbal seasoning to taste
½ cup chopped green part of leeks (optional)

Combine all the ingredients in a large saucepan. Bring to a boil and simmer for 20 minutes. Strain. Discard the bones. (I like to bury them in the garden. The tomato plants there love them.) The fish scraps can be made to make a salad or fish cakes.

Easy-Broiled Cod

Flounder, sole, scrod, or any other lean fish can be substituted for the cod. This is quick and easy and extremely low in calories.

4 fish fillets (about 1¼ pounds)
herbal seasoning and freshly ground pepper, to taste

2 tablespoons butter
1 tablespoon fine fresh bread crumbs (preferably whole grain)
1 tablespoon sesame seeds

Preheat the broiler to high. Sprinkle the fish with herbal seasoning and pepper. Set aside.

In an oven-proof casserole large enough to hold the fish in one layer, add the butter and heat under the broiler until butter melts. Add the fish fillets and turn them over to coat both sides with butter. Combine the bread crumbs and sesame seeds. Sprinkle the fish evenly with this mixture.

Place the coated fish under the broiler about 5 inches from the source of heat. The thickness of the fish will determine the cooking time. A very thin fillet such as that of a small sole or flounder will cook in about 2 to 4 minutes. A one-inch-thick cod will need about 8 minutes.

Yield: 4 servings. *Each serving provides: 168 cal, 18 g pro, 4 g sat fat, 3 g unsat fat, 58 mg sodium, 50 mg chol.*

Zesty Baked Halibut in Mustard Sauce

2 pounds halibut steak
2 tablespoons butter
2 tablespoons whole-wheat
  pastry flour
1 cup milk
2 teaspoons prepared mustard
1 tablespoon canola or olive
  oil

4 medium-size onions, sliced
1 teaspoon herbal seasoning
¼ teaspoon freshly ground
  pepper
1 quart boiling water
  acidulated with 1
  tablespoon lemon juice or
  white vinegar

In a saucepan or skillet, melt 2 tablespoons of butter, add the flour, and blend with a fork or whisk. Slowly add the milk while cooking on low heat, until the mixture thickens. Add the mustard, herbal seasoning, and pepper.

In another saucepan or skillet, heat the oil and cook the onion slices until golden and transparent.

Slip the halibut into the boiling acidulated water and simmer for 3 minutes. Drain and set aside.

In a shallow baking dish, spread the cooked onions; place the drained halibut on top of the onions. Pour the mustard sauce over all. Bake about 20 minutes at 425 degrees.

Yield: 6 servings. *Each serving provides: 190 cal, 22.8 g pro, 2.5 g sat, fat, 3.2 g unsat fat, 84 mg sodium, 50 mg chol.*

Red Snapper Fillets with Potatoes and Tomato-Chili Sauce

Serve with a crisp green salad and you've got a wholesome, satisfying meal!

3 pounds red snapper fillets
(cod or other firm fish
fillets may be substituted)
½ teaspoon dried oregano
¼ cup lemon juice

16 small potatoes, steamed
1½ cups Tomato-Chili Sauce
(recipe follows)
½ cup sliced almonds or
sunflower seeds

In an oven-proof baking dish, arrange fish in a single layer. Sprinkle with oregano and lemon juice, cover tightly, and bake at 350 degrees for 5 to 10 minutes, depending on the thickness of the fish.

When fish is no longer translucent and flakes easily with the tines of a fork, place it on a heated platter. Arrange the potatoes around the fish. Cover with the Tomato-Chili Sauce. Sprinkle with sliced almonds or sunflower seeds.

TOMATO-CHILI SAUCE

2 cups tomatoes, coarsely
chopped
1 tablespoon canola or olive
oil

⅛ teaspoon cinnamon
⅛ teaspoon ground cloves
3 jalapeno or green chilis,
chopped

In a saucepan, combine the tomatoes and oil. Cook for 5 minutes. Add remaining ingredients and simmer for 5 more minutes.

Yield: 6 servings. *Each serving, urith sauce, provides: 210 cal, 20 g pro, 0 g sat fat, 2 g unsat fat, 230 mg sodium, 40 mg chol.*

Halibut Balls (Gefilte Fish)

One time when we were fishing off my brother's boat, one of our kids threw his line in and said, "I hope I can catch a gefilte fish." Of course he didn't, but whatever fish he hooked could be made into gefilte fish. The word "gefilte" means stuffed. Originally, the preparation described here was intended as a stuffing, usually for carp or pike. The original purpose was to make a little fish go a long way. But, because of its unique taste appeal, gefilte fish has become a staple in Jewish cuisine, especially for Sabbath and holiday meals. Various kinds of fish may be included in the mixture, but haddock or halibut gives the fish a firm texture. Don't forget the horseradish.

2 *pounds halibut or haddock, or a combination, skin and bones removed*
1 *medium-size onion*
2 *eggs*
3 *tablespoons wheat germ or oat bran or a combination*

½ *cup fish stock or water herbal seasoning and pepper to taste*
1 *large onion, sliced*
1 *large carrot, sliced*

Put fish and onion through a food grinder or in the food processor, using the steel blade. Process until ingredients are well chopped, but

(continued)

225

not puréed. Add the eggs, wheat germ or oat bran, fish stock or water, and seasonings and process till ingredients are well blended.

Place the sliced onion and carrot in the bottom of a large pot or soup kettle. With moistened hands, form the fish mixture into "golf balls" and place them in the pot. Add fish stock or water to cover the fish. Cover pot and cook over low heat for about 1½ hours or until fish balls are tender.

Yield: 12 servings. *Each serving provides: 108 cal, 17.4 g pro, .2 g sat fat, 7.2 g unsat fat, 94 mg sodium, 97 mg chol.*

Crunchy Pecan Fish Fillets

A royal dish, you can prepare this when you get home from the office and have it ready for an early dinner for family or special guests. Pecans, with their high content of iron, magnesium, potassium, vitamins A, C, and E, and polyunsaturated fats, contribute to your zest for living. I prefer grinding the nuts myself to the purchased crumbs, which very often are rancid.

2 tablespoons milk
3 tablespoons prepared
    mustard

4 fish fillets (especially good
    with scrod, haddock, or
    orange roughy)
1 cup ground pecans

In a small bowl, combine milk and mustard. Dip the fillets into this mixture, then into the ground pecans. Shake off excess. Place on a baking sheet, greased with butter or sprayed with non-stick cooking spray, and bake at 500 degrees for 10 to 12 minutes, or until fish flakes easily.

Yield: 4 servings. *Each serving provides: 281.5 cal, 23.4 g pro, 1.5 g sat fat, 16.2 g unsat fat, 188 mg sodium, 47 mg chol.*

Broiled Fish Kabobs

Who needs hot dogs? Enjoy this marvelous picnic dish for backyard or patio entertaining. Try cooking the corn, unhusked, in the microwave for about 10 minutes. Cool and husk. Use 6 fish fillets (try perch, bass, tile, or halibut). Corn provides vitamin A, potassium, magnesium, some vitamin C—and the lovely taste of summer.

6 *fish fillets*
3 *cobs of corn, cooked*
2 *red peppers, cut into 2-inch
    pieces*
3 *tablespoons canola or olive
    oil*
3 *tablespoons low-sodium
    soy sauce*
½ *cup finely chopped onion*
⅓ *cup lemon juice*

2 *cloves garlic, minced*
¼ *teaspoon Tabasco® sauce*
1 *cup whole-grain bread
    crumbs*
1 *teaspoon herbal seasoning*
1 *lemon or lime, cut in
    wedges*
  *cooked brown or wild rice,
    or a combination*

Cut fish into 2-inch pieces. Cut each ear of corn into 4 pieces. In a large shallow bowl, combine fish, corn, red pepper, oil, soy sauce,

(*continued*)

lemon juice, herbal seasoning, garlic, and Tabasco®. Mix well. Cover and refrigerate at least an hour, stirring occasionally.

When ready to serve, preheat the broiler. Drain the fish and vegetables. Reserve the marinade. Roll the fish pieces in the bread crumbs. Thread the fish, vegetables, and lemon or lime wedges, alternating, on 6 skewers about 16 inches long. Place the skewers on a greased broiler pan about 10 inches from the source of heat. Broil for 8 to 10 minutes, turning skewers and basting with the marinade, until fish flakes easily. Serve the kabobs over the rice.

Yield: 6 servings. *Each serving, with ½ cup brown rice, provides: 368 cal, 29 g pro, 1 g sat fat, 6 g unsat fat, 366 mg sodium, 47 mg chol.*

Black Sea Bass Fillets

The firm, white juicy black sea bass is not a stranger to you if you ever ordered steamed fish at a Chinese restaurant. Remember how delectable it was? You can enjoy this lean delicacy (only 2 percent fat) at home on a bed of succulent vegetables and spices. On the West Coast, black sea bass changes its name to rockfish and may even change its color to shades ranging from green to orange to red. Because black sea bass is seasonal, it's not always available at the fish market. Red snapper fillets are a good substitute.

1 tablespoon olive or canola
   oil
½ cup chopped onion
2 cloves garlic, minced
1 cup finely chopped leeks
1 cup chopped ripe tomatoes
½ cup finely chopped celery or
   fennel
1 teaspoon turmeric
½ cup dry white wine
1 cup fish broth

1 bay leaf
4 sprigs fresh thyme or 1
   teaspoon dried
⅛ teaspoon cayenne pepper
1 teaspoon herbal seasoning
⅛ teaspoon freshly ground
   pepper
6 black sea bass fillets (about
   2¼ pounds)
3 tablespoons chopped
   coriander or parsley

In a saucepan, heat the oil. Add the onion, garlic, tomatoes, celery or fennel, and turmeric. Cook, stirring over medium heat, for about 3 minutes, or until vegetables are wilted. Add the wine, fish broth, bay leaf, thyme, cayenne pepper, vegetable seasoning, and pepper. Bring to a boil and simmer 10 minutes.

In a large skillet arrange the fillets in one layer. Remove the bay leaf from the tomato sauce and pour the sauce over the fish. Cover and simmer for about 5 minutes, or until it flakes easily. Sprinkle with parsley or coriander.

Yield: 6 servings. *Each serving provides: 177.5 cal, 19.3 g pro, .3 g sat fat, 4 g unsat fat, 92 mg sodium, 41 mg chol.*

Pollack in Cream

Pollack is a first cousin to cod and haddock. It tastes like its cousins but is a more substantial member of the family; the flesh of pollack is firmer and more chewy. However, it may be substituted for haddock or cod and vice versa. In this recipe the pollack is baked in cream, which makes a luscious sauce. You can use some of the sauce on your baked potato and eliminate the butter, or you can substitute milk for the cream.

1½ pounds fillet of pollack
2 tablespoons lemon juice
1 teaspoon prepared mustard
½ teaspoon Worcestershire
   sauce
1 teaspoon herbal seasoning

¼ teaspoon freshly ground
   pepper
3 small onions, quartered
1 cup light cream
   parsley and paprika

Wipe the fish with a damp cloth and place in an oven-proof casserole. Combine the lemon juice, mustard, Worcestershire sauce, herbal seasoning, and pepper. Pour this mixture over the fish. Add the onions and the cream.

Bake in a 400-degree oven for about 15 minutes, or until fish flakes easily. Garnish with parsley and sprinkle with paprika.

Yield: 6 servings. *Each serving provides: 214 cal, 20.9 g pro, 7 g sat fat, 7.1 g unsat fat, 75 mg sodium, 50 mg chol.*

Butter-Broiled Snapper

A snap to prepare, it has a delectable, succulent flavor.

1½ pounds snapper fillets
2 tablespoons unsalted butter, melted
¼ cup lemon juice

½ cup whole-grain bread crumbs
1 teaspoon herbal seasoning
¼ teaspoon freshly ground pepper

Brush the fish with the butter and lemon juice. Coat the fish with the bread crumbs combined with the herbal seasoning and pepper. Broil for 5 to 8 minutes, or until fish flakes easily with a fork.

Yield: 6 servings. *Each serving provides: 180 cal, 21 g pro, 6 g sat fat, 5.6 g unsat fat, 126 mg sodium, 40 mg chol.*

Beautiful Baked Fish Fillets

1 pound fish fillets (flounder, sole, etc.)
1 cup plain yogurt
2 tablespoons finely chopped onion
2 tablespoons finely chopped green or red pepper
2 tablespoons chopped dill pickle
1 tablespoon chopped parsley
1 tablespoon lemon juice
¼ teaspoon dry mustard
paprika
lemon slices
1 ripe avocado, pitted, peeled, and sliced

Arrange fish in a baking dish. In a small mixing bowl, combine yogurt, onion, pepper, pickle, parsley, lemon juice, and mustard. Spread the yogurt mixture over the fish. Sprinkle with paprika. Bake at 375 degrees for about 15 minutes, or until fish flakes easily. Garnish with lemon slices and avocado slices.

Yield: 4 servings. *Each serving provides: 192 cal, 23.9 g pro, 3.6 g sat fat, 9.9 g unsat fat, 89 mg sodium, 45 mg chol.*

Baked Grouper, Mediterranean Style

The grouper, a large and low-fat fish, is known as the "Chameleon of the Sea." It not only changes its color to match its surroundings, it can actually paint its own stripes when near other, threatening fish. But even more fascinating is the sex life of the grouper. (Talk show hosts would love them.) They are all female at birth, and change their sex at a later age. They are cousins to the bass family and can be used interchangeably. A savory blend of flavors and colors is this grouper recipe, which delights the eye and the taste buds. The orange provides vitamin C, which helps you to metabolize important minerals. It is also one of the antioxidants that have been shown to retard the development of malignancies.

2 tablespoons olive oil
2 tablespoons lemon juice
1 tablespoon fresh oregano
    leaves or ½ teaspoon dried
1 teaspoon finely shredded
    orange zest
2 pounds grouper fillets

1 teaspoon herbal seasoning
¼ teaspoon freshly ground
    pepper, or to taste
thick slices of orange or
    orange wedges
¼ cup small black olives
    (optional)

Heat oven to 350 degrees. In a shallow baking dish, large enough to hold the fish in a single layer, combine the oil, lemon juice, oregano, and orange zest. Place the fish fillets in the dish and turn them to coat with the oil and lemon mixture. Sprinkle with herbal seasoning and pepper.

Place in the oven and bake for 20 to 25 minutes or until the fish is opaque and tender in the center when flaked with a fork. Baste with the pan juices several times during the baking period. Garnish with the orange pieces and the olives.

Yield: 6 servings. *Each serving, with olives, provides: 166.4 cal, 19.73 g pro, .2 g sat fat, 6 g unsat fat, 341.5 mg sodium, 50 mg chol.*

Tilapia

Tilapia is a warm-water fish native to the Nile and other rivers in the Middle East. Maybe you know it as St. Peter's fish. When you buy tilapia today, chances are it never came near the Middle East but was raised in heat-controlled water tanks, fed and fattened with pellets of grains, vitamins, and minerals, and then placed in clean water without food for three to five days to get rid of any offensive fishy flavor. Then it traveled to the bed of ice in your fish market. (This is aquaculture.)

Tilapia are farm-raised in Florida, California, Maryland, and Pennsylvania. The largest production sites, Solar Aqua Farms, a corporate partner of Chiquita Brands International in Sun City, California, distributes as much as 15,000 pounds a week all over the country. For those concerned with the hazards of ocean pollution, aquaculture represents safe harbor. In fact, the demand for the fish is so great that producers say they cannot keep up with it.

Tilapia promises to become the "fish of the future," not only for its safety but for its white, delicate, moist flesh, which picks up the flavors of sauce and seasoning and cooks up in less than 5 minutes.

If tilapia is not yet in your local market, ask the manager of the fish department if it can be stocked. Until it is available to you, use flounder, sole, or orange roughy in the following recipes.

Lemon-Broiled Herbed Tilapia

Have a party. Serve this recipe with lovely Almond-Acorn-Squash Bowls (halved acorn squash stuffed with cooked brown rice, raisins, and chopped toasted almonds, and baked).

2 teaspoons canola or olive oil
2 tablespoons lemon juice
1 garlic clove, crushed
⅛ teaspoon dried thyme or oregano

2 tilapia fillets (3 to 6 ounces each)
pepper to taste
2 teaspoons chopped parsley

Preheat boiler.

Combine 1 teaspoon oil with lemon juice, garlic, and thyme or oregano.

If you're not using a non-stick broiler pan, line it with foil, then place the lined broiler pan 2 inches from the heat and preheat it for 2 to 3 minutes.

Rub one side of each fillet with oil and lay it in a heated broiling pan, oiled side down. Spoon about two-thirds of the lemon juice mixture over the fillets and broil 5 to 10 minutes, depending on the thickness of the fish (an inch-thick fillet will take 10 minutes). Baste twice, using lemon juice mixture and pan juices.

Remove from the broiler, transfer to warm plates, and spoon pan juices over fillets. Sprinkle each fillet with pepper and chopped parsley.

Yield: 2 servings. *Each serving provides: 200 cal, 30 g pro, 1 g sat fat, 8 g unsat fat, 100 mg sodium, 40 mg chol.*

Baked Tilapia with Sweet Spices and Tangy Dressing

You'll enjoy this lovely medley of flavors.

1 *teaspoon ground ginger*
¼ *teaspoon nutmeg*
¼ *teaspoon cinnamon*
1 *teaspoon ground cumin*
¼ *teaspoon cayenne pepper*

2 *teaspoons minced garlic*
4 *tilapia (about 2½ pounds total)*
2 *teaspoons olive or canola oil*
Orange-Onion Relish

In a small bowl, combine the ginger, nutmeg, cinnamon, cumin, cayenne, and garlic. Wash the tilapia and dry with absorbent paper. Rub the inside cavities with the spice mixture.

Arrange the fish in a shallow glass baking dish and brush with the oil. Cover lightly with foil and bake in a preheated 400-degree oven for about 15 minutes, or until flesh is opaque when tested with a fork. Serve with Orange-Onion Relish.

Yield: 4 servings. *Each serving, without the relish dressing, provides: approximately 117 cal, 21 g pro, 1 g sat fat, 6 g unsat fat, 100 mg sodium, 50 mg chol.*

ORANGE-ONION RELISH

2 *medium-size oranges, peeled, seeded, and diced*

¼ *cup red onion, finely chopped*
2 *tablespoons salad dressing*

In a small bowl, combine oranges and onion. Stir in the salad dressing.

Yield: about 1 cup, or 4 servings. *Each serving provides: 51 cal, 1.4 g pro, practically no fat, sodium, or cholesterol.*

Lightly Sautéed Garlic-Flavored Tilapia

4 tilapia fillets (3½ ounces
    each)
2 tablespoons lemon juice
    herbal seasoning and
    pepper

1 teaspoon olive or canola oil
2 teaspoons butter
1 teaspoon minced garlic
1 tablespoon chopped parsley

Wash fillets and pat dry with absorbent paper. Sprinkle with lemon juice, herbal seasoning, and a little pepper.

In a large non-stick skillet, heat the oil and butter. Sauté the fish for 2 to 3 minutes on each side, or until nicely browned. Remove from the skillet and place on a heated platter.

Stir the garlic and parsley into the pan juices and heat. Spoon the garlic sauce over the fish.

Yield: 4 servings. *Each serving provides: 125 cal, 21 g pro, 1.5 g sat fat, 6 g unsat fat, 40 mg sodium, 50 mg chol.*

21

THE FATTER FISH
(6 to 20 percent Omega-3 Fatty Acid Content)

When a fish is called "fatty," it is not an insulting sobriquet. It means that it has a more pronounced flavor and, because it has over 6 percent fat, it is easily broiled without any additional fat. But, more important, it means that it provides more wonder-working Omega-3's than its cousins on the lean side.

When cooking fatty fish, remember that, unlike lean fish, it needs few additions to keep it moist and flavorful. A touch of flavored vinegar, lemon, lime, or orange juice enhances the flavor while it mellows the taste. The best way to preserve the Omega-3's is to broil, bake, poach, or steam the fish.

The recipes for fatty fish in this section can be used interchangeably for bluefish, butterfish, mackerel, ocean perch, pompano, salmon, shad, or tuna.

Salmon, King of Fish

If the fish of all the rivers, lakes, and oceans held a popularity contest, which one do you think would swim down the runway wearing the crown and throwing kisses? No doubt about it, salmon wins the crown. In fact, Izaak Walton, author of *The Compleat Angler,* dubbed salmon "king of fish"; indeed, one of the most popular varieties is called king salmon.

Salmon's unique rich and meaty flavor is love at first bite, no matter how you choose to serve it—poached, broiled, grilled, smoked, or baked . . . as steaks, fillets, whole or out of a can.

Whether it swims in the Atlantic or Pacific, salmon is high in protein and, compared to other fish, is high in fat. But even the fattest has less fat than chicken or steak, and what fat it does have is unsaturated and a superior source of the wonder-working Omega-3 fatty acids.

There are some differences between the salmon of the Atlantic and their cousins in the Pacific. Atlantic salmon is pink and comes to market fresh. Pacific salmon comes in many forms. It may come in cans, smoked or fresh, and the varieties include the prized king, also called chinook, which comes from Alaska and the Columbia River area. Other varieties from the Pacific include the red-fleshed sockeye, pinkish-silvery coho, and yellow-tinted dog (salmon which has very little fat).

Canned salmon is practically a staple in every home. Why not? It is so versatile and so good-tasting. You've probably noticed the price differential between the costly squat cans and the more economical tall cans. That's because the squat can contains the most desirable part, cut from the center, while the tall can houses the tail meat.

When using canned salmon, be sure to include the bones and skin. Simply mash them up. They are a wonderful source of calcium.

The recipes that follow will help you to enjoy the wonderful flavor and health benefits of succulent salmon.

Salmon Salad with Gingery Raisin Sauce

Serve it hold or cold as a salad on a bed of greens and shredded carrots, or serve it with a baked potato and steamed broccoli. However you serve it, dress it up with the delicious raisin sauce included in this recipe.

1 tablespoon arrowroot or cornstarch
1 cup orange juice
½ cup raisins
2 tablespoons sliced green onion
2 teaspoons Dijon mustard

1 teaspoon grated fresh ginger or ⅓ teaspoon powdered
1 teaspoon chopped fresh dill weed
¼ teaspoon herbal seasoning
4 salmon steaks (about 1½ pounds)

Mix the cornstarch with 2 tablespoons of the orange juice. Add it to the remaining orange juice and bring it to a boil, stirring until thickened. Stir in the raisins, onion, mustard, ginger, dill, and herbal seasoning. Mix well and set aside.

Place the fish in a buttered baking dish. Place the oven rack about 6 inches below the source of heat. Broil for 5 to 8 minutes on each side. To test for doneness, see if you can remove the center bone without taking any of the flesh with it.

To serve as a salad, place each steak atop a bowl of salad greens and shredded carrots. Drizzle with the raisin dressing.

Yield: 4 servings. *Each serving provides: 262 cal, 20 g pro, 4.4 g fat, 5.2 g unsat fat, 53 mg sodium, 66 mg chol.*

Grilled Whole Salmon with Ginger and Lime

Salmon is a great fish for grilling, because it won't dry out too much. Make sure the grill is very clean and very hot. In lieu of a grill, you could use a double thickness of oiled foil with lots of holes punched in it, to allow the smoke to come through.

¾ cup (6 ounces) reduced--calorie cream cheese
½ cup plain yogurt
1 tablespoon chopped candied ginger or ginger marmalade
grated rind of 1 lime
3- to 4-pound whole salmon, cleaned and scaled, head and tail intact

canola or peanut oil for greasing the grill and lubricating the fish
freshly ground pepper to taste
1 lime, sliced
about 1 teaspoon ground ginger, or to taste

To make the sauce, mix together the cheese, yogurt, candied ginger or ginger marmalade, and lime zest in a small bowl.

To grill the salmon, brush the salmon—inside and outside—with the oil. Sprinkle with pepper and ginger. Put the lime slices in the cavity of the fish. Brush the grill with oil. Place the fish on the grill. Cook for 10 minutes. Brush again with oil and, with a spatula, carefully turn it. Continue cooking for 8 to 10 minutes, or until the fish flakes easily when tested with a fork.

Using the spatula, transfer the salmon to a serving platter. Serve the hot salmon with the room-temperature lime-ginger sauce.

Yield: 6 servings. *Each serving provides: 265 cal, 23 g pro, 28 g sat fat, 19 g unsat fat, 110 mg sodium, 70 mg chol.*

Broiled Marinated Salmon Steaks

Halibut, tuna, or swordfish may be substituted for the salmon in this quick-and-easy recipe.

2 tablespoons canola or olive oil

⅓ cup wine or balsamic vinegar

1 teaspoon Worcestershire sauce

freshly ground pepper, to taste

1 bay leaf

2 tablespoons chopped parsley

2 tablespoons chopped fresh dill or 1 teaspoon dried

1½ pounds salmon cut in 1-inch-thick steaks

In a shallow bowl, combine the oil, vinegar, Worcestershire sauce, pepper, bay leaf, dill and parsley. Add the fish steaks. Cover and refrigerate for at least 3 hours, turning occasionally.

Remove from marinade and place on a buttered or foil-covered broiler pan. Baste with the marinade. Place the broiler pan about 3 inches from the heat source. Broil about 10 minutes, or until fish flakes easily when tested with a fork. Baste with the sauce before serving.

Yield: 6 servings. *Each serving provides: 193 cal, 18 g pro, 1.5 g sat fat, 3.6 g unsat fat, 175 mg sodium, 58 mg chol.*

Honey and Ginger Salmon Fillet

If you have any of the honey-ginger sauce left over from the following recipe, it makes a lovely salad dressing.

1 tablespoon honey
1 tablespoon finely grated
   fresh ginger or ½
   teaspoon ground
3 tablespoons lemon juice
1 teaspoon sodium-reduced
   soy sauce

1 teaspoon minced parsley
1½ pound salmon fillet
1 teaspoon herbal seasoning
¼ teaspoon freshly ground
   pepper, or to taste

In a small bowl, combine the honey, ginger, lemon juice, soy sauce, and parsley.

Place the salmon in an oven-proof baking dish, buttered, oiled, or sprayed with non-stick cooking spray. Spread with about half of the honey-ginger mixture. Sprinkle with herbal seasoning and pepper.

Bake in a preheated 425-degree oven for 10 minutes per inch of thickness. About halfway through the cooking period, spread over the fish the remaining honey-ginger sauce.

Yield: 6 servings. *Each serving provides: 159 cal, 21.6 g pro, 2.63 g sat fat, 3 g unsat fat, 97 mg sodium, 52 mg chol.*

Poached Salmon

This is an elegant dish to set before the king. Notice that there is no fat needed in the preparation of poached fish. The court bouillon that remains in the poacher can be refrigerated or frozen and used again.

water to fill fish poacher
halfway
2 cups dry white wine
2 tablespoons peppercorns
1 tablespoon herbal seasoning
2 onions, sliced

½ cup white wine vinegar
1 cup chopped celery with the
tops included
5- to 6-pound whole salmon or
one that fits your poacher
lemon slices

Place the water, wine, peppercorns, herbal seasoning, onions, vinegar, and celery in the poacher and boil for 15 minutes. Strain the mixture (it's now called a court bouillon) and let it cool to room temperature.

Wash the salmon; make sure the scales are removed; and trim off all of the fins. Check to see if the salmon fits the poacher. If it's a bit too long, trim off a little of the tail. With a ruler, measure the thickest part of the fish and take note of it. Wrap the fish in cheesecloth and place it in the poacher over high heat. When the court bouillon begins to boil, begin timing the cooking. It should cook for 10 minutes per inch of thickness. A 2-inch-thick fish should cook for 20 minutes. For every tenth of an inch more, figure another minute.

Remove the fish promptly to a warm platter. Carefully remove the cheesecloth. Serve triumphantly with a yogurt and dill sauce on the side or any of the sauces suggested in the foregoing recipes. Garnish with lemon wedges.

Yield: 10 servings. *Each serving, without the sauce, provides: 180 cal, 20 g pro, 4 g sat fat, 6.4 g unsat fat, 45 mg sodium, 66 mg chol.*

YOGURT-DILL SAUCE

1 cup yogurt
1 teaspoon grated onion

3 tablespoons minced fresh
    dill
1 teaspoon lemon juice

In a small glass bowl, combine all ingredients.

Yield: 1 cup. *One tablespoon provides: 9.5 cal, .5 g pro, .5 g sat fat, 7 mg sodium.*

Salmon Mousse

After unmolding, go creative. Use a black olive for an eye, sprigs of dill for fins, and lemon half-slices for scales. This never fails to make a hit.

1 tablespoon unflavored
   gelatin
¼ cup cold water
½ cup boiling water
½ cup reduced-calorie
   mayonnaise
1 tablespoon lemon juice
¼ teaspoon cayenne pepper
1 tablespoon grated onion

1 teaspoon herbal seasoning
¼ teaspoon paprika
¼ teaspoon nutmeg
2 cups chopped-up cooked
   salmon pieces
½ cup heavy cream, whipped
sprigs of dill
lemon slices

Soften the gelatin in the cold water. Add the boiling water. Stir to dissolve gelatin, then cool. Add the mayonnaise, lemon juice, cayenne pepper, grated onion, herbal seasoning, paprika, and nutmeg. Mix well. Chill the mixture to the consistency of raw egg white. Add the salmon and mix well. This can be done in the food processor, using the steel blade. Fold the whipped cream into the salmon mixture.

Oil a fish mold. Add the salmon mixture. Refrigerate the mold until the mixture is set. Unmold on a serving platter and garnish with sprigs of dill and lemon slices. Serve with Yogurt-Dill sauce from the preceding recipe.

Yield: 8 servings. *Each serving provides: 174 cal, 12 g pro, 4.9 g sat fat, 7 g unsat fat, 43 mg sodium, 66 mg chol.*

Grilled Salmon on a Roll

What a great dish for a patio supper or picnic! Your guests will bless you.

3 salmon steaks (each about 1 inch thick)
1 tablespoon canola or olive oil
3 tablespoons lemon juice
1 teaspoon herbal seasoning
½ teaspoon freshly ground pepper
6 sandwich rolls, preferably whole grain, cut in halves, crosswise
romaine lettuce leaves
cucumber slices

Brush both sides of the salmon steaks with the oil. Sprinkle with lemon juice, herbal seasoning, and pepper. Let them rest for 10 minutes.

Grease the grill with cooking spray or brush it with oil. Place the salmon in the center of grill over hot coals and allow to cook for 10 minutes, turning them once. On the side of the grill, lightly toast the split rolls.

Divide the salmon into 6 portions. Remove any skin and bones. Place a lettuce leaf and cucumber slices on bottom halves of the rolls. Place salmon on top and cover with the top halves.

Yield: 6 servings. *Each serving provides: 292 cal, 24.8 g pro, 4.7 g sat fat, 6 g unsat fat, 285 mg sodium, 66 mg chol.*

Carolyn's Salmon-Noodle Kugel with Mushrooms

This is a tasty meal in a dish, wonderful to have on hand when unexpected guests drop in. It freezes well.

1 can (7¾ ounces) or 1 cup flaked leftover salmon

1 8-ounce package medium-size noodles, cooked

1 tablespoon butter

1 cup sliced mushrooms

3 tablespoons chopped green onion

2 tablespoons wheat germ or oat bran

½ cup plain yogurt

1 cup cottage cheese

1 tablespoon chopped dill

1 tablespoon chopped parsley

1 tablespoon sesame seeds

Flake the salmon. Cook and drain the noodles. In a large skillet, melt the butter and lightly sauté the mushrooms and onion. Stir the wheat germ or oat bran into the pan. Add the yogurt. Heat the mixture but do not allow it to boil. Add the cottage cheese, dill, and parsley.

Combine the cheese mixture with the salmon and cooked noodles. Place the mixture in a greased 8 x 10-inch oven-proof casserole. Sprinkle with sesame seeds. Bake at 350 degrees for 20 to 25 minutes in a conventional oven, or 8 to 10 minutes in the microwave.

Yield: 6 servings. *Each serving provides: 254 cal, 19 g pro, 4.3 g sat fat, 2 g unsat fat, 245 mg sodium, 80 mg chol.*

Variation: Especially for the kids. Make a Salmon-Noodle Pizza. Simply top with a half-cup of grated part-skim mozzarella cheese before baking.

Salmon Soufflé

Delicately delicious, this dish provides a powerhouse of nutrients.

1 can (7¾ ounces) salmon or
   1 cup leftover salmon
1 cup milk, including liquid
   from salmon
2 tablespoons butter
2 tablespoons whole-wheat
   flour

1 teaspoon herbal seasoning
¼ teaspoon freshly ground
   pepper
¼ teaspoon dry mustard
1 tablespoon minced parsley
3 eggs, separated

If you're using canned salmon, drain it and reserve the liquid. Add milk to the salmon liquid to total 1 cup. If you're using leftover salmon, use 1 cup milk.

In a skillet, melt the butter, blend in the flour, herbal seasoning, pepper, and dry mustard. Add the milk mixture, and cook, stirring constantly, until thickened and smooth. Add the salmon and parsley. Beat the egg yolks. Slowly add the salmon mixture to the yolks, mixing thoroughly.

Beat egg whites stiff but not dry. Fold the egg whites gently into the salmon mixture. Turn into an ungreased 1-quart soufflé dish. Bake at 350 degrees for 30 to 40 minutes, or until brown and puffy. Serve immediately.

Yield: 4 servings. *Each serving provides: 257 cal, 18.8 g pro, 7 g sat fat, 4.6 g unsat fat, 380 mg sodium, 210 mg chol.*

Crispy Oven-Fried Salmon

Oven-frying is a healthy substitute for deep-fat frying. The result is a moist interior and a deliciously crunchy outside.

1 pound fish fillets (salmon or any kind)
2 tablespoons reduced-calorie mayonnaise

5 tablespoons whole-grain bread crumbs
1 teaspoon parsley flakes
½ teaspoon paprika

Coat fish on both sides with mayonnaise. Combine bread crumbs, parsley flakes, and paprika. Coat the fillets with this mixture. Place in a shallow glass casserole dish. Bake at 450 degrees for 12 minutes.

Yield: 4 servings. *Each serving provides: 221 cal, 21.7 g pro, 2 g sat fat, 3.6 g unsat fat, 88 mg sodium, 66 mg chol.*

Shad, the Harbinger of Spring

When shad makes its appearance in the fish markets, you know it's time to put away the snow shovel and look for daffodils on the hill. Shad is a most welcome harbinger of spring. Enjoy it frequently when it's in season. It won't be around very long. It has a most delectable flavor, and comes to us from unpolluted water. It will neither swim nor spawn in polluted waters.

Because shad has an elaborate bone structure, it was considered "trash fish" for many years, before a workable system for removing those bones was devised. It is now generally available as boned fillets.

If you'd like to bake a whole shad, try the first of the following recipes.

Whole Shad

Using this method, the bones will soften but they will not disappear.

1 whole shad (about 3
    pounds)
juice of 1 lemon

dry white wine, enough to
    cover the fish

Marinate the fish in the wine combined with the lemon juice, for several hours or overnight. Make sure the wine-lemon combo covers the fish.

To bake the fish, place it in an oven-to-table baking pan. Pour the marinade over it. Bake in a moderate oven, about 350 degrees for 10 minutes, per inch of fish, measured at its thickest point. If the fish measures 2½ inches thickness, allow 25 minutes baking time.

Yield: 6 servings. *Each serving provides: 180 cal, 20 g pro, 3 g sat fat, 6.6 g unsat fat, 200 mg sodium, 70 mg chol.*

Grilled or Broiled Marinated Herb-Flavored Shad

1 fillet of shad
1 teaspoon herbal seasoning
¼ teaspoon freshly ground
   pepper
2 tablespoons olive or canola
   oil
2 tablespoons lemon juice

½ teaspoon finely crumbled
   bay leaf
1 tablespoon fresh thyme or
   ½ teaspoon dried
¼ teaspoon paprika
   lemon or lime wedges

Place the fillet, skin side down, in a baking dish. Sprinkle with the herbal seasoning and the pepper.

In a small dish, combine the oil, lemon juice, bay leaf, and thyme and spread over and around the fish. Cover and let stand in the refrigerator for 2 hours.

Preheat the broiler to high. Spread the fish with paprika. Place under broiler about 4 inches from the source of heat and broil for 5 minutes. Cut the fish in half, lengthwise. Place on hot serving dishes. Spoon a little marinade over each serving. Serve with lemon or lime wedges.

Yield: 2 servings. *Each serving provides: 190 cal, 18.6 g pro, 2 g sat fat, 12 g unsat fat, 150 mg sodium, 370 mg chol.*

Baked Shad without Bones

This fish provides lots of good calcium because you eat bones and all. The bones dissolve during the long baking period. You may find some dilution of the flavor. The potatoes and onions make a very pleasant counterpoint to the flavor of the fish.

1 whole shad (about 3 pounds)
2 tablespoons vinegar
5 medium-size potatoes, scrubbed and sliced
4 medium-size onions, sliced
1 teaspoon herbal seasoning
½ teaspoon freshly ground pepper

Cut gashes about ¼ inch apart along both sides of the shad. Place the shad on a large piece of aluminum foil or parchment paper. Sprinkle the vinegar all over the fish. Surround the fish with the potatoes and onions. Sprinkle all with pepper and the herbal seasoning.

Fold and seal the foil or parchment paper and place in a baking pan. Bake 6 hours in a 300-degree oven. The little bones will soften and crumble like the bones in canned salmon. Everything is edible except the backbone.

Yield: 6 to 8 servings. *Each serving (of 6), with potatoes and onions, provides: 171 cal, 22.8 g pro, 3 g sat fat, 6.6 g unsat fat, 207 mg sodium, 70 mg chol.*

Shad with Tomatoes and Mushrooms

1 boneless fillet of shad
½ teaspoon herbal seasoning
¼ teaspoon freshly ground
    pepper
¼ cup milk
½ cup whole-grain flour
2 tablespoons canola or olive
    oil

2 cups sliced mushrooms
1 teaspoon finely minced
    garlic
1 tablespoon butter
½ cup canned tomatoes,
    crushed
2 tablespoons finely chopped
    parsley

Split fillet in half, crosswise. Sprinkle with half of the herbal seasoning and pepper. Place in a small flat bowl with the milk. Remove fish pieces from the milk without draining. Place the dripping fish pieces in the flour and coat both sides.

Heat the oil in a skillet. Add the fish pieces, skin side up. Cook about 1½ minutes over high heat or until golden brown. Carefully turn and continue cooking on the other side over moderately low heat for 3 to 4 minutes. Transfer the fish to two warm serving plates.

Heat the oil in the skillet. Add mushrooms, herbal seasoning and the remaining pepper. Cook, stirring, about 2 minutes. Add garlic and butter. Stir until butter melts.

In a small saucepan, heat the tomatoes and cook down for about 5 minutes. Spoon half of the tomatoes onto each piece of fish. Pour mushrooms over all, and sprinkle with parsley.

Yield: 2 servings. *Each serving provides: 400 cal, 25.5 g pro, 8 g sat fat, 14 g unsat fat, 258 mg sodium, 80 mg chol.*

Shad Roe

Fish roe consists of thousands of tiny, unfertilized eggs clustered together and enclosed in two sacs. It is very rich in vitamins and minerals and low in fat. The Indians fed it to weaning babies as a nourishing substitute for mother's milk.

Shad roe is the most popular of the species, but the roe of other fish are also tasty and nourishing. Caviar is the processed roe of the sturgeon. It is very expensive and much too salty for my taste buds. But the roe of other fish—salmon, cod, pike, flounder, tuna, herring, carp, and shad—are also delectable, not nearly so expensive, and certainly less salty.

Shad roe is at its most flavorful when the eggs are small and dark red. Fresh shad roe should be firm to the touch, not soft or mushy. It can be prepared in many different ways and presents an entirely new taste sensation with each procedure.

Shad Roe in Buttery Lemon Sauce

2 pairs of shad roe
1 cup milk
½ cup whole-wheat flour
4 tablespoons unsalted butter
2 tablespoons olive or canola oil
1 tablespoon dry white wine

2 tablespoons chopped chives or scallions
2 tablespoons lemon juice
1 teaspoon herbal seasoning
½ teaspoon freshly ground pepper
lemon or lime slices for garnish

Soak the shad roe in milk for about 10 minutes. Drain and pat dry. Spread the flour on wax paper. Dredge the roe in the flour.

In a 12-inch skillet, heat 2 tablespoons butter and 2 tablespoons oil. Sauté the floured roe until golden brown, about 6 minutes on each side. Remove from the skillet and keep warm.

Add the wine to the sauce in the skillet and heat, scraping the tasty morsels from the bottom of the pan. Add chives and the remaining 2 tablespoons butter. Heat until the butter is golden brown. Stir in the lemon juice, herbal seasoning, and pepper. Pour the sauce over the shad roe. Garnish with lemon or lime slices and serve immediately.

Yield: 4 servings. *Each serving provides: 262 cal, 15 g pro, 7.8 g sat fat, 14.9 g unsat fat, 42 mg sodium, chol N.A. (not available).*

Nancy's Shad Roe Salad

2 cups water
1 slice lemon
1 tablespoon cider vinegar
1 pair of shad roe

1 cup chopped celery
1 small cucumber, chopped
and chilled

DRESSING

1 tablespoon horseradish
2 tablespoons lemon juice
¼ cup mayonnaise
½ cup plain yogurt

½ teaspoon herbal seasoning
¼ teaspoon freshly ground
pepper

Combine the water, lemon, and vinegar in a saucepan. Add the fish roe and simmer for about 20 minutes. Remove to a wire rack to drain, then chill it in the refrigerator. After it is chilled, cut it into cubes.

To make the dressing, combine the horseradish, lemon juice, mayonnaise, yogurt, herbal seasoning, and pepper. Add the chopped celery and cucumber. Last, add the cubed shad and toss, being careful not to break up the roe.

Yield: 4 servings. *Each serving provides: 191 cal, 13.7 g pro, 2 g sat fat, 1.5 g unsat fat, 41.15 mg sodium, chol N.A. (not available).*

Trout

Trout is a smallish fish, weighing in at 1 to 5 pounds. Unless you have snared your own catch, the rainbow trout you're having for dinner has been farm-raised.

A moderately fatty fish, trout is delicious whether it is steamed, broiled, baked, grilled, or sautéed. It is an excellent source of Omega-3 fatty acids, which have been shown to have a preventive effect against coronary heart disease.

Delight your taste buds and your heartstrings with the following recipes.

Broiled Rainbow Trout

So easy to prepare, so moist and delicious! Serve with steamed broccoli topped with chopped roasted walnuts and herbed brown rice.

4 small trout, pan-ready

¾ cup low-calorie Italian dressing or your own dressing made with olive oil, vinegar, garlic, and herbs

Marinate the trout in the dressing for at least 30 minutes. Broil 4 inches from source of heat for 10 minutes per inch of thickness, measured at its thickest part.

(continued)

After 5 minutes of cooking time, brush the fish with the marinade, turn and continue broiling until the fish flakes easily when tested with a fork.

Yield: 4 servings. *Each serving provides: 267 cal, 24.9 g pro, 4 g sat fat, 6.37 g unsat fat, 52 mg sodium, 50 mg chol.*

Trout, Hardly Cooked

Undercooked fish is nutritionally superior—moist, sweet, and very delicious. Try this way of preparing it.

4 *small trout, or as many as*	½ *cup yellow cornmeal*
you have mouths to feed	1 *teaspoon canola or olive oil*

Place the cornmeal on a sheet of wax paper. Turn the fish in the cornmeal to coat both sides.

Heat a skillet large enough to hold the fish in a single layer. Add the oil; put in the trout. Let the cornmeal brown very lightly, then turn the fish and turn off the heat. Leave the fish in the skillet just long enough to heat through but not cook. Serve at once, browned side up, with wedges of lemon.

Yield: 4 servings. *Each serving provides: 226 cal, 26 g pro, 3 g sat fat, 3.87 g unsat fat, 52 mg sodium, 50 mg chol.*

Barcelona Trout Fillets

You get an intermingling of fine flavors when you cook the whole meal in one skillet.

1 teaspoon olive or canola oil
1 cup brown rice
½ cup minced celery
½ cup minced onion
⅓ cup chopped parsley
3 cloves garlic, minced
1 tablespoon fresh thyme or ½ teaspoon dried

2 cups vegetable or fish stock, or water
1 pound trout fillets
3 chopped plum tomatoes or ½ cup canned tomatoes
½ cup green peas or mung bean sprouts

In a large skillet, heat the oil. Add the rice, celery, onion, parsley, garlic, paprika, and thyme. Sauté for 3 to 4 minutes, stirring constantly. Add the stock. Bring to a boil, then reduce heat. Cover and simmer for 25 minutes.

Add the fillets and simmer for 8 more minutes. Add the tomatoes and peas or sprouts. Simmer long enough to heat the peas or sprouts (about 2 minutes). Arrange attractively on a heated platter.

Yield: 4 servings. *Each serving, including the vegetables, provides: 403.6 cal, 26.9 g pro, 3.58 g sat fat, 6.27 g unsat fat, 109 mg sodium, 50 mg chol.*

Sautéed Trout

Serve with whole-wheat dinner rolls and a salad of grated carrots and zucchini sprinkled with balsamic vinegar—and you have a romantic dinner for two.

1 trout (about 1 pound)
¼ cup low-calorie Italian
 dressing or your own,
 made with olive oil,
 vinegar, and herbs

1 slice whole-grain bread,
 made into crumbs
¼ cup oat bran
1 teaspoon butter
1 teaspoon olive or canola oil

Rinse the fish under cold running water and pat dry with paper towels. Place the fish in a shallow bowl and add the dressing. Turn the fish to coat all sides. Leave it in the marinade for 15 minutes. Spoon the dressing over it several times. In a separate bowl, or on a double piece of wax paper, place the bread crumbs, mixed with the oat bran. Dredge the fish in this mixture, then refrigerate about 5 minutes. This will help the crumbs to "set."

In a heavy skillet, heat the oil and butter. Sauté fish until golden on one side; turn and continue to cook for a total time of 10 minutes per inch of thickness, measured at the fish's thickest part. If the fish is less than 1 inch at its thickest part, cook only until it flakes easily when tested with a fork.

Yield: 2 servings. *Each serving provides: 240 cal, 28 g pro, 4 g sat fat, 3.87 g unsat fat, 60 mg sodium, 50 mg chol.*

Mackerel

When the mackerel make their first appearance of the season on the fish counter, you know it must be spring. Their high fat content enables them to take the winter off and just hibernate.

When fresh, mackerel have a lovely blue-green iridescence. Their flavor is distinctive and slightly gamey—which is why it tastes best when prepared with a slightly acidic sauce. Compared to the cost of other fish on the market, mackerel gives your wallet a break. And, of all fish, mackerel has the highest proportion of Omega-3 fatty acids, which have been shown to lessen the incidence of coronary heart disease.

Most mackerel hang out in northern waters and in the Mediterranean. The big daddy of the family, the kingfish—more accurately known as the king mackerel, weighing in at as heavy as 70 pounds—likes to winter down south, around both the eastern and western coasts of Florida.

Good "stand-ins" that can be substituted for mackerel in the following recipes are bluefish, butterfish, trout, and fresh herring.

Swedish Grilled Mackerel

This treat fills the air with an appetite-teasing aroma.

4 mackerel (¾ to 1 pound
   each)
2 tablespoons olive or canola
   oil
1 tablespoon lemon juice
½ cup chopped onion
1 teaspoon Dijon mustard

2 tablespoons chopped dill
1 tablespoon chopped chives
1 teaspoon herbal seasoning
½ teaspoon freshly ground
   pepper
2 tablespoons butter, melted

Place the washed-and-dried fish in a shallow glass dish.

In a small bowl, combine the oil, lemon juice, onion, mustard, dill, chives, herbal seasoning, and pepper. Pour the marinade over the fish and allow fish to marinate for 1 hour, turning them once.

Place the fish on oiled grill. Brush both sides of the fish with the melted butter. Grill 3 inches above the white-hot coals for 4 minutes. Turn and grill the flip side for 6 minutes or until fish flakes easily when tested with a fork.

Yield: 4 servings. *Each serving provides: 256 cal, 21.9 g pro, 6 g sat fat, 12 g unsat fat, 101 mg sodium, 40 mg chol.*

Baked Mackerel with Vegetables

Here is a wholesome, economical meal to serve a merry party of eight. The vinegar cuts the high-fat flavor of the fish. The vegetables provide fiber, vitamins, and minerals.

two	2-pound mackerel	¾	cup wine vinegar
	fish stock or water	1	tablespoon chopped parsley
1	large onion, chopped	¼	teaspoon dried thyme
1	large carrot, sliced	1	bay leaf
½	green pepper, chopped		

Wash the fish and dry with paper towels. Place them in a shallow glass baking dish, lined with parchment paper or sprayed with non-stick cooking spray.

In a saucepan, combine the onion, carrot, pepper, and vinegar. Mix thoroughly; then add the parsley, thyme, and bay leaf. Add just enough fish stock or water to cover. Simmer for 10 minutes. Remove the bay leaf.

Pour the sauce over the fish. Bake in a 400-degree oven for about 15 to 20 minutes, or until fish flakes easily when tested with a fork. Serve fish and sauce in the dish you baked them in.

Yield: 8 servings. *Each serving provides: 162 cal, 11.4 g pro, 2 g sat fat, 5.3 g unsat fat, 96 mg sodium, 40 mg chol.*

Mackerel Salad

Canned mackerel makes it possible to enjoy the flavor and health values of this fish when it isn't available in the marketplace. It also provides a meal that doesn't put a dent in your wallet. Mackerel is canned with water, and salt is added. If you are on a low-salt diet, rinse the fish with cold water before combining it with the other ingredients.

2 tablespoons white wine, tarragon, or balsamic vinegar

1 teaspoon Dijon mustard

1 clove garlic, minced

1 tablespoon olive or canola oil

2 tablespoons minced parsley

2 tablespoons snipped chives or scallions

¼ cup chopped red onion

1 teaspoon minced fresh tarragon or ¼ teaspoon dried

one 15-ounce can of mackerel, drained and flaked (Crush the bones. Do not discard them. They are an excellent source of calcium.)

1 cup thinly sliced cucumbers or radishes, or a combination

1 head romaine or Boston lettuce

1 cup watercress leaves or parsley

In a medium-size glass bowl, combine the vinegar, mustard, garlic, and oil. Whisk to blend ingredients. Stir in the parsley, chives or scallions, and red onion. Add the mackerel and toss gently. Cover and refrigerate for about an hour.

When ready to serve, add the radishes or cucumbers to the mackerel. Line a large salad plate with romaine or Boston lettuce, torn in bite-size pieces and combined with the watercress leaves or parsley. Place the mackerel salad on the greens. Garnish with parsley sprigs.

Yield: 4 servings. *Each serving provides: 150 cal, 11.4 g pro, 3 g sat fat, 7.3 g unsat fat, 90 mg sodium, 40 mg chol.*

Bluefish

A member of the sea bass family, bluefish is a beautiful, feisty fish that weighs in at 2 to 25 pounds. It is named for the bluish-gray tint of its full-flavored, slightly sweet flesh that takes well to acidic sauces. It is high in protein, moderately fatty, and a good source of the wonder-working Omega-3 fatty acids.

Mackerel can be substituted for bluefish in the following recipes.

Baked Bluefish Fillets with
Peppers and Tomatoes

The tomatoes and vinegar provide just enough acidity to cut through the fat in the bluefish.

2 pounds bluefish fillets
1 teaspoon olive or canola oil
½ cup chopped green pepper
1 16-ounce can stewed tomatoes
1 teaspoon red wine vinegar

¼ teaspoon coarsely ground coriander seeds
1 teaspoon Dijon mustard
¼ teaspoon freshly ground pepper

Wash the fillets and dry with absorbent paper. Place them in a shallow glass baking dish.

In a skillet, heat the oil and sauté the peppers briefly. Add the tomatoes, vinegar, coriander, mustard, and pepper. Stir and spoon over the bluefish. Bake in a 400-degree oven for 12 to 15 minutes, or until flesh flakes easily when touched with a fork.

Yield: 6 servings. *Each serving provides: 247 cal, 21.1 g pro, 2.4 g sat fat, 6.2 g unsat fat, 172 mg sodium, 59 mg chol.*

Curried Bluefish with Zucchini and Yogurt

Here's a dieter's delight: a lovely high-fiber, low-calorie meal in a dish!

1 teaspoon olive or canola oil
1 large onion, chopped
2 cups thinly sliced zucchini
1 tablespoon curry powder
½ teaspoon freshly ground
   pepper

2 pounds bluefish fillets
1 cup plain yogurt
¼ cup minced green onion
2 tablespoons sesame seeds
½ teaspoon paprika

Spray a large, non-stick skillet with non-stick cooking spray. Heat 1 teaspoon oil. Add onion, zucchini, curry powder, and pepper. Stir and cook over moderate heat for about 10 minutes. Set aside.

Spray with non-stick cooking spray a shallow glass baking dish large enough to accommodate the fish in a single layer.

Drain the zucchini mixture, reserving the drained-off liquid. Add this liquid to the yogurt along with the minced onion. Combine the zucchini mixture with the yogurt mixture and spread it evenly over the fish. Sprinkle with the sesame seeds. Dust with the paprika. Bake in a 400-degree oven for about 15 minutes, or until fish flakes easily when tested with a fork.

Yield: 6 servings. *Each serving provides: 165 cal, 22.6 g pro, 2.9 g sat fat, 3.5 g unsat fat, 70.5 mg sodium, 59 mg chol.*

Tuna

We're all familiar with the flavor and convenience of canned tuna. Over a billion cans are sold annually in the United States. The largest member of the mackerel family, some tuna weigh in at 1,000 pounds—most of which goes directly to the cannery.

Fortunately, some of that tuna will bypass the cannery and go directly to the fish markets, where it is available to you. And believe me, if you've never tried fresh tuna, you're missing out on a simply sensational food experience, as well as a most delicious source of protein, vitamins, and minerals. Here are several different ways to prepare it.

Tuna Steaks with Ginger and Garlic

I like to serve with these as side dishes a high-fiber combo of brown and wild rice and steamed cauliflower.

2 *tablespoons minced ginger root*
4 *large cloves of garlic, minced*
2 *tablespoons dry white wine*
2 *tablespoons sodium-reduced soy sauce*

1 *teaspoon herbal seasoning*
½ *teaspoon freshly ground pepper*
¼ *teaspoon honey*
4 *tuna steaks, about ½ inch thick*

In a Pyrex baking dish large enough to accommodate the steaks in one layer, combine the ginger root, garlic, wine, soy sauce, herbal seasoning, pepper, and honey. Add the tuna steaks. Let them marinate for 15 minutes, turning them over several times.

Place the steaks in a preheated broiler or grill and grill for about 2 minutes on each side, or until just cooked through. Do not overcook. Serve immediately on heated plates.

Yield: 4 servings. *Each serving, without the side dishes, provides: 180 cal, 30.24 g pro, .12 g sat fat, .12 g unsat fat, 85 mg sodium, 63 mg chol.*

Tuna Burgers

Serve these at your next patio picnic. Your weight-watching, health-minded guests will bless you. You can make the ginger juice by grating a 2-inch piece of fresh ginger.

1½ pounds fresh tuna, finely chopped
1 teaspoon ginger juice
3 tablespoons finely minced red onion
1 teaspoon reduced-sodium soy sauce
1 tablespoon chopped cilantro or parsley

1 tablespoon olive or canola oil
½ teaspoon Tabasco®
1 teaspoon herbal seasoning
¼ teaspoon freshly ground pepper
1 teaspoon oil for brushing burgers and grill

(continued)

In a bowl, combine the tuna with the ginger juice, minced onion, soy sauce, cilantro or parsley, oil, Tabasco®, herbal seasoning, and pepper. Shape the mixture into 4 patties and place in freezer for about 10 minutes.

Brush the burgers on both sides with oil and oil the grill. Grill over high heat for 2 minutes. Turn carefully and grill the other side for 1 minute, or until the burgers are seared on the outside. They will be almost raw on the inside. Serve on toasted burger rolls with lettuce, tomatoes, and lemon wedges.

Yield: 4 servings. *Each serving, without the roll, provides: 205 cal, 35 g pro, 1.12 g sat fat, 6.12 g unsat fat, 50 mg sodium, 63 mg chol.*

Barbecued Tuna with Balsamic Vinegar

This is a most savory dish. Serve it with pasta and a salad.

2 *tuna steaks, about 5 ounces each, or one large steak cut in half*
1 *tablespoon olive oil*
2 *tablespoons balsamic vinegar*

¼ *cup fresh cilantro or parsley, finely chopped*
1 *clove garlic, minced*
1 *teaspoon herbal seasoning*
¼ *teaspoon freshly ground pepper, or to taste*
oil for the grill

Rinse the tuna, then poke several holes on both sides to aid in absorbing the marinade.

Make a marinade by combining the oil, vinegar, cilantro or parsley, garlic, herbal seasoning, and pepper. Place the tuna in a small bowl and pour the marinade over it. Let it marinate for 20 minutes.

Brush the grill with oil to prevent sticking. When the grill is hot, drain the tuna and place it on the grates for 1 minute. Lift the tuna and make a quarter-turn on the same side. This will help prevent the fish from sticking, and will make an attractive cross-hatch pattern on the steaks. Grill 3 more minutes, then turn over and repeat the process.

Yield: 2 servings. *Each serving provides: 185 cal, 35 g pro, 1.12 g sat fat, 6.12 g unsat fat, 40 mg sodium, 63 mg chol.*

Swordfish

Even if you are an avid fisherman, I doubt that you'll ever find a swordfish nibbling at your bait. They can weigh up to 600 pounds. But you may find luscious swordfish steaks in your fish market. Its flesh is firm, dense, and flavorful (reminiscent of veal).

Swordfish takes well to marinades and lusty seasoning. It is wonderful grilled, broiled, baked, or stir-fried.

The following recipes will help you expand your swordfish horizons.

Parks' Swordfish with Lemon-Rosemary Marinade

We enjoyed this succulent dish at Parks' Seafood, in Allentown, Pennsylvania, my favorite restaurant. Fred Parks, owner and creative genius, graciously shared this recipe with me.

1 tablespoon shallots	½ teaspoon onion salt
2 tablespoons olive oil	¼ teaspoon dried tarragon
2 tablespoons dry white wine	¼ teaspoon dried rosemary
1½ tablespoons lemon juice	6 swordfish steaks
½ teaspoon ground white pepper	(approximately 2 ½ to 3 pounds total)

In a skillet, sauté the shallots lightly in the heated oil. Add the wine, lemon juice, ground white pepper, onion, salt, tarragon, and rosemary. Heat just till warm in order to extract the flavors. Cool to room temperature; then marinate the steaks in it for approximately 20 minutes.

Using two wide spatulas, transfer the swordfish to an oiled baking dish large enough to hold them without overlapping.

Bake at 400 degrees for 10 minutes per inch of thickness, measured at the thickest part, or until fish flakes easily when touched with a fork. Baste with the marinade several times during the baking process.

Yield: 6 servings. *Each serving provides: 185 cal, 19.4 g pro, 3 g sat fat, 7.4 g unsat fat, 90 mg sodium, 50 mg chol.*

Grilled Swordfish Citron

And now for a medley of delectable flavors . . .

½ cup orange juice
¼ cup lemon juice
1 tablespoon olive oil
1 teaspoon herbal seasoning
1 ½-inch piece fresh ginger,
    peeled and minced

1 large clove garlic, minced
⅛ teaspoon cayenne pepper
6 swordfish steaks (5 to 6
    ounces each)

To grill, prepare a hot charcoal fire.

Meanwhile, combine the juices, oil, herbal seasoning, ginger, garlic, and cayenne in a shallow glass casserole. Mix till well blended. Marinate the swordfish in this at room temperature for 20 minutes, turning several times.

Place the fish on an oiled cooking grid set about 4 inches above the hot ashes. Grill for 6 minutes, then turn, brush with marinade, and grill for about 4 minutes longer, or until fish flakes easily when touched with a fork.

Yield: 6 servings. *Each serving provides: 203 cal, 21 g pro, 2 g sat fat, 5 g unsat fat, 50 mg sodium, 50 mg chol.*

Stir-Fried Swordfish with Water Chestnuts

This recipe also works well with other firm-flesh fish such as salmon, tile, or tuna. Serve with hot brown rice studded with chopped, toasted almonds.

1 cup vegetable or fish broth
1 tablespoon reduced-sodium soy sauce
1 tablespoon cornstarch
¼ teaspoon hot pepper sauce
2 tablespoons olive or canola oil
2 teaspoons finely chopped fresh ginger root

1 large clove of garlic, minced
1 8-ounce can of water chestnuts, drained and sliced
2 cups broccoli florets
1 pound fresh swordfish, cut into 1-inch chunks

In a small bowl, combine the broth, soy sauce, cornstarch, and hot pepper sauce. Set aside.

In a non-stick skillet or wok, heat the oil; add the ginger and the garlic. Cook and stir briefly (about 30 seconds). Add the drained and sliced water chestnuts and the broccoli; cook, stirring, for about 2 minutes. Add the swordfish chunks; continue cooking and stirring until fish is opaque.

Stir the sauce into the skillet or wok. Reduce heat to medium; cook covered for 2 minutes longer, until fish is just fork tender and broccoli is bright green, crisp, and tender.

Yield: 4 servings *Each serving provides: 260 cal, 26 g pro, 4 g sat fat, 8 g unsat fat, 250 mg sodium, 50 mg chol.*

22

MISCELLANEOUS FISH

Gefilte Fish

Maybe you've never tasted gefilte fish, but you are most certainly acquainted with Tevye and his devotion to "tradition" as depicted in the popular musical *Fiddler on the Roof.* While Tevye was singing, Golda was chopping. With a big wooden bowl in her lap and a metal cleaver in her hand, she was chop-chop-chopping the carp, pike, and buffalo: She was making gefilte fish for the Sabbath meal.

Tradition lives. In Jewish homes all over the world, gefilte fish is a traditional Sabbath and holiday specialty. But you don't have to be Jewish to relish a piece of gefilte fish smothered in sinus-clearing horseradish.

Of course, some things change. You can now buy it in jars or cans, some with salt, some with sugar, some jelled, some with all-white fish, some with a mixture of fish. But there's nothing like the kind that Momma made, the kind you make yourself. "Hard on the chopping arm, but good for the soul," my mom used to say.

When selecting the fish, consider fish with three different qualities: fat, dry, and flaky. Traditional choices are carp, pike, white, and, of course, a little buffalo. When you ask for buffalo, the fishmonger might direct you to the meat department. Actually, what Momma called buffalo is a freshwater bass with a little mouth. I guess it has the visage of a buffalo. (It is not generally available.)

Momma's Gefilte Fish

Various kinds of fish can be used. Polish-style gefilte fish calls for haddock, cod, or whiting. The haddock is desirable because it contributes to a firmer texture. Adding the onion skins gives the broth a lovely color. My Mom used carp, pike, whiting, and, when she could find it, buffalo (she called it buffel).

3 pounds fish (carp, pike, or whiting)
2 onions, grated (reserve 2 pieces of onion skin)
2 carrots, grated
2 eggs
2 teaspoons herbal seasoning
½ teaspoon white pepper
½ cup water
3 tablespoons ground almonds or whole-wheat bread crumbs
2 onions, sliced
2 carrots, sliced
water

Fillet the fish or have it filleted at the fish market. Retain the skin, bones, and heads. Using a grinder or food processor, puree the fish fillets. Remove this to a wooden chopping bowl. Using a single-blade chopper with a handle, continue chopping the mixture as you add

278

the onions, carrots, eggs, 1 teaspoon herbal seasoning, ¼ teaspoon white pepper, water, and ground almonds or bread crumbs. The mixture should feel just slightly sticky.

In a large heavy pot or poacher, place the bones, heads, and skin in the bottom. Add the sliced onions, sliced carrots, 2 cups water, 1 teaspoon herbal seasoning, the remaining ¼ teaspoon white pepper, and the onion skins. Cover the pot, bring to a boil, then lower heat and simmer for about 20 minutes.

Meanwhile, with moistened hands, shape the fish into ovals about 3 inches long and 1¼ inches in diameter and place them on wax paper. Bring the broth to a smiling roll and lower the fish into the broth. Make sure the boiling liquid almost covers the fish. If necessary, add another ½ cup water. Lower the heat and simmer on a very low flame for 2 hours. Let cool in the broth.

Using a slotted spoon, remove the cooled fish to a serving dish. Remove the carrots and garnish each piece of fish with a slice of carrot.

Cook down the stock to concentrate it, adjust the seasonings, then spoon a little over the gefilte fish. Leave to "set," and serve cold with horseradish.

Yield: about 12 pieces. *Each piece provides: 150 cal, 14.5 g pro, .3 g sat fat, .9 g unsat fat, 68 mg sodium, 10 mg chol.*

Tuna Gefilte Fish

For those occasions when time is pressing, or the budget is tight, this Tuna Gefilte Fish is ideal.

1 can (7½ ounces) white-meat tuna
2 eggs
1 grated onion (reserve the skin)
2 tablespoons wheat germ

herbal seasoning and white pepper
4 cups water
2 medium-size onions, sliced
2 carrots, sliced
⅛ teaspoon white pepper
1 teaspoon herbal seasoning

In a food processor, purée the tuna, eggs, grated onion, and wheat germ. Season to taste with herbal seasoning and white pepper. Form into ovals or balls.

In a large pot, combine the water, sliced onions, sliced carrots, white pepper, and herbal seasoning. Bring to a boil, then reduce heat and simmer for 20 minutes. Place the tuna balls into the stock. Cover and simmer over low heat until the vegetables are soft—about 30 minutes. Allow the fish to cool in the stock.

With a slotted spoon, remove the fish to a platter. Place a slice of carrot on each. Concentrate the stock, then pour some over the fish. Serve with horseradish.

Yield: 8 appetizer servings. *Each serving provides: 90 cal, 9 g pro, 1.2 g sat fat, 1.5 g unsat fat, 30 mg sodium, 30 mg chol.*

Seafood Linguine

If you avoid shellfish for religious reasons or because you question its safety, there are some new products on the market that mimic that taste and texture but are actually made from pollack, a fin fish. Sometimes these are called "Sea Legs." Another of the brands available is called "It's Not Crab!—It's Kosher Fish." It is pre-cooked and can be used in any recipe that calls for canned tuna; or you can use canned tuna for this linguine.

1 teaspoon olive or canola oil
1 teaspoon butter
2 medium-size tomatoes, cubed
2 green onions, sliced
4 cloves garlic, minced
½ cup chopped parsley
12 ounces of "It's Not Crab!" or "Sea Legs"

2 tablespoons lemon juice
2 tablespoons fresh thyme, chopped, or 1 teaspoon dried
½ teaspoon freshly grated pepper
1 package linguine, cooked and drained

In a large non-stick skillet, heat the oil and butter. Gently sauté the tomatoes, onions, and garlic for about 2 minutes. Do not let the garlic brown. Stir in the parsley, fish, lemon juice, thyme, and pepper. Simmer for another 2 minutes. Stir in the cooked linguine. Can be enjoyed hot or cold.

Yield: 8 servings. *Each serving provides: 240 cal, 22 g pro, 2.5 g sat fat, 5 g unsat fat, 17 mg sodium, 41 mg chol.*

Smoked Fish

My friend Arnie Lichtman is a master of the art of smoking fish and, I must admit, Arnie's fish has a marvelous flavor.

How do you prepare smoked fish? If you have an outdoor grill—no problem.

First, soak two handfuls of hickory chips in water. Then, start a charcoal fire. When the coals are glowing and covered with gray ash, take a few hickory chips, shake off excess water, and add them to the hot coals.

Brush the grill and the fish with oil or spritz them with nonstick cooking spray. Place the fish, skin side down, on the greased grill over the coals. Cover and smoke for 20 minutes to an hour, depending on the thickness of the fish, or until fish flakes easily and has a pleasant smoked aroma and flavor.

During the smoking process, add hickory chips to the fire to keep up a steady supply of smoke.

Now invite the neighbors—or your extended family—to share the feast. All cares and worries go up in smoke!

Smoked Salmon

Even if you don't have access to an outdoor grill, you can enjoy smoked fish. I used salmon for this dish, but you can use bluefish, mullet, perch, pompano, pike, tuna, or just about any kind available. Use a heavy cast-iron Dutch oven. Line the bottom with several layers of aluminum foil crimped up to about 1 inch off the bottom. Place the smoking ingredients on top of this platform. The ingredients you select depend on the flavors you wish to capture. Here's what I used.

2 teabags (any strong-flavored tea)	zest of one orange
	2 ¼-inch slices ginger root
3 sprigs thyme	1 cinnamon stick
3 sprigs oregano	2 tablespoons brown rice

Put the lid on the Dutch oven and raise the heat to "high." When it begins to smoke, about 3 minutes, set a steamer basket that's been spritzed with non-fat cooking spray over the smoke and put the rinsed and dried fish in it. Put the lid on and allow it to smoke for about 10 minutes.

Remove the Dutch Oven from the burner and let it sit for about 5 minutes. Serve with brown rice flavored with a bit of saffron or turmeric for a lovely golden color.

Marinade for Smoked Fish

This very tasty marinade can be used for any fish, even one prepared by methods other than smoking.

¼ cup balsamic or red-wine vinegar
½ teaspoon cinnamon
¼ teaspoon powdered cloves
½ teaspoon grated ginger root or ¼ teaspoon powdered

2 tablespoons low-sodium soy sauce
freshly grated nutmeg
¼ teaspoon freshly ground pepper

Combine all ingredients and pour over the fish. Let the fish marinate for about 30 minutes. Then follow the procedure for smoking fish.

23

ACCOMPANIMENTS: SIDES AND SAUCES

The side dishes and sauces you serve with your fish should also be "smart." That means, of course, that they must contribute nutrients as well as flavor, and not throw a monkey wrench into your efforts at weight control.

Here are some of my favorites.

Horseradish Sauce

This is a satisfying, lusty complement to your broiled, baked, or sautéed fish. It's also a lovely salad dressing.

1 cup yogurt
2 tablespoons prepared
    horseradish (red or white)

2 tablespoons minced green
    onion or chives

Combine all ingredients in a pretty glass bowl. Refrigerate for at last 30 minutes to give flavors a chance to meld.

Yield: a little more than 1 cup. *Each tablespoon provides: 8.4 cal, .5 g pro, .1 g sat fat, .1 g unsat fat, 9 mg sodium, 0 mg chol.*

Creole Sauce

This sauce doubles as a zingy salad dressing.

1 onion, chopped
1 large tomato, chopped
1 hot pepper, chopped
2 garlic cloves, finely minced
1 teaspoon herbal seasoning

¼ teaspoon freshly ground
    pepper
    juice of 1 lime
2 teaspoons olive or canola oil
    fresh parsley

In a bowl, combine all the ingredients. Let the mixture stand at room temperature for about one hour. Serve raw, with lightly sautéed or poached fish.

Yield: about 1½ cups or about 8 servings. *Each serving provides: 19 cal, .4 g pro, .2 g sat fat, .5 g unsat fat, 1 mg sodium, 0 mg chol.*

Sweet Potato in Orange Baskets

A beautiful side dish, this is rich in flavor and nutrients, especially beta-carotene and vitamin C—two very important anti-oxidants.

8 oranges
1 pound sweet potatoes, boiled, baked, or microwaved, peeled and mashed
2 large eggs
1 cup milk
grated zest and juice of 1 lemon
2 tablespoons molasses or honey

Cut the top quarter off each orange, then hollow oranges with a grapefruit scorer or a melon-baller.

In a bowl, blend the scooped-out orange segments with the sweet potatoes, eggs, milk, lemon, and molasses or honey.

Fill each orange shell with the sweet-potato mixture. Bake for 20 minutes.

Yield: 8 servings. *Each serving provides: 97 cal, 4 g pro, 1 g sat fat, .9 g unsatfat, 56 mg sodium, 60 mg chol.*

Barley-Mushroom Casserole

Here's a truly delectable gourmet casserole to serve with fish. Barley is believed to be the first grain utilized by man. Pearled barley lacks the bran and germ of the original grain, so it cannot qualify as a whole grain. But a North Dakota organic farmer has made available his hull-less (it grows that way) unpearled barley; that's the kind I used in the preparation of this dish.

1 teaspoon herbal seasoning	½ pound mushrooms, sliced
2 cups cooked barley	¼ teaspoon freshly ground
2 teaspoons olive or canola oil	pepper
½ cup chopped onion	¼ teaspoon sage
¼ cup chopped green pepper	

Stir the herbal seasoning into the barley. Set aside.

In a skillet, heat the oil and lightly sauté the onions, pepper, and mushrooms, stirring occasionally. Stir in the pepper, sage, and cooked barley. Cook over low heat for 5 more minutes.

Place the barley mixture in a 1½-quart casserole. Bake, uncovered, in a preheated 350-degree oven for 25 minutes. Serve hot as an accompaniment to fish.

Yield: 6 servings. *Each serving provides: 126 cal, 3.7 g pro, .5 g sat fat, .3 g unsat fat, 16 mg sodium, 0 mg chol.*

Pistachio Pasta Salad with Oregano Dressing

Oregano means "joy of the mountain." This salad will bring joy to your taste buds.

6 ounces rotini or shell macaroni	1 cup chopped tomato
boiling water	1 cup blanched pea pods
Oregano Dressing	¼ cup chopped shelled pistachios
2 cups torn fresh spinach	Parmesan cheese (optional)

Cook the rotini or macaroni in the boiling water according to package directions. Drain.

To make the dressing, simply combine all ingredients.

OREGANO DRESSING

¼ cup olive oil	¾ teaspoon crushed dried oregano
¼ cup red-wine vinegar	⅛ teaspoon garlic powder

Marinate the hot rotini or macaroni in the Oregano Dressing. Cool to room temperature. Combine with spinach, tomato, pea pods, pistachios, and pepper. Sprinkle with Parmesan cheese, if you choose to use it.

Yield: 8 servings. *Each serving provides: 100 cal, 4 g pro, .4 g sat fat, .5 g unsat fat, 11.5 mg sodium, 0 mg chol.*

Mandarin Rice Pilaf

This is a wonderful partner for a fish dinner. It takes a little longer to prepare, but the delight with which it is always received justifies the extra effort. Make it for a special occasion—or just make it, and dinner will be special.

1 tablespoon olive or canola oil
1 onion, finely chopped
2 cups raw brown rice
2 cups orange juice
2 cups boiling water
12 whole cloves
1 small piece stick cinnamon (about 2 inches)
¼ teaspoon powdered ginger
3 tangerines or oranges, sectioned
½ cup raisins
¼ cup sliced toasted almonds

In a large saucepan, heat oil and sauté onions until soft. Add rice and continue cooking for 5 minutes, stirring constantly. Add orange juice to boiling water; pour the liquid over the rice. Add cloves, cinnamon, and ginger.

Cover and simmer for 35 minutes, or until liquid is absorbed. Remove cloves (count them) and cinnamon stick. Stir in the orange or tangerine sections, reserving 6 for garnish. Stir in the raisins.

Place the rice in a serving dish and garnish with the reserved fruit and toasted almonds.

Yield: 8 servings. *Each serving provides: 255 cal, 5 g pro, 1.1 g sat fat, 1.3 g unsat fat, 11 mg sodium, 0 mg chol.*

Potato Kugel

You can exercise your arm muscles and grate the vegetables by hand, or you can use the food processor and prepare the mixture in jig time.

2 cups raw potatoes, unpeeled, scrubbed, grated, and drained
1 large onion, grated
1 large carrot, grated
2 eggs, beaten
¼ cup wheat germ
¼ cup oat bran
1 teaspoon herbal seasoning
1 teaspoon baking powder
⅛ teaspoon freshly grated pepper
3 tablespoons olive or canola oil

In a large bowl, mix together the potatoes, onion, carrot, eggs, wheat germ, oat bran, herbal seasoning, baking powder, pepper, and 2 tablespoons of the oil.

Place the mixture in a well-greased and preheated 9 x 9-inch baking dish. Sprinkle the remaining oil over the top. Bake in a 375-degree oven for about 1 hour, or until top is crisp and brown.

Yield: 8 servings. *Each serving provides: 106 cal, 4 g pro, .5 g sat fat, 9.2 g unsat fat, 19 mg sodium, 0 mg chol.*

Fried Green Tomatoes

This recipe is adapted from one by the Whistle Stop Café.

1 medium-size green tomato
   herbal seasoning
   freshly grated pepper, to
     taste

½ cup cornmeal
2 tablespoons canola or olive
   oil

Slice tomatoes about ¼ inch thick, season with herbal seasoning and pepper, and then coat both sides with cornmeal.

In a large skillet, heat the oil. Sauté the tomatoes until lightly browned on both sides.

Alternate method: Instead of frying, place the sliced and coated tomatoes in a greased baking dish. Sprinkle each slice with a few drops of oil, or spritz with cooking spray, and bake in a 350-degree oven for about 15 minutes.

Yield: 2 servings. *Each serving provides: 175 cal, 3.5 g pro, 1 g sat fat, 6 g unsat fat, 2.17 mg sodium, 0 mg chol.*

INDEX

Ask for these Jane Kinderlehrer titles at your local bookstore or order today.

Use this coupon or write to Newmarket Press, 18 East 48th Street, New York, NY 10017 (212) 832-3575.

Please send me:

The Smart Baking Cookbook—Muffins, Cookies, Biscuits, and Breads

More than 180 recipes for heavenly, healthful muffins, cookies, biscuits, breads, and toppings—high in fiber and protein and low in fat, sodium, and cholesterol. Plus, instructions on wheat-, sugar-, and dairy-free baking.

"Kinderlehrer knows how to strike a balance between taste and nutrition that will have diners clamoring for more." —*Publishers Weekly*

___ $16.95, paperback, 304 pages (ISBN 1-55704-522-4)
___ $21.95, hardcover, 304 pages (ISBN 1-55704-281-0)

The Smart Chicken & Fish Cookbook—Over 200 Delicious and Nutritious Recipes for Main Courses, Soups, and Salads

Delectable fish and fowl recipes for main courses, soups, and salads—all high-fiber, low-fat, low- or no-sugar, low sodium, and low cholesterol.

"[Kinderlehrer] not only steers you to delicious and nutritious eating, but also gives you the facts you need to be informed." —*The International Cookbook Revue*

___ $16.95, paperback, 320 pages (ISBN 1-55704-544-5)

For postage and handling, add $3.50 for the first book, plus $1.00 for each additional book. Please allow 4-6 weeks for delivery. Prices and availability subject to change.

I enclose a check or money order, payable to Newmarket Press, in the amount of $_____ .

Name _____

Address _____

City/State/Zip _____

Clubs, firms, and other organizations may qualify for special discounts when ordering quantities of these titles. For more information, please call or write Newmarket Press, Special Sales Department, 18 East 48th Street, New York, NY 10017; call (212) 832-3575; fax (212) 832-3629; or e-mail mailbox@newmarketpress.com.

www.newmarketpress.com